# DIESELS

## IN THE

## WHITE ROSE COUNTY

Although London King's Cross is far removed from the lines in Yorkshire, the train headboard is an appropriate introduction to this volume. The photograph depicts the prototype English Electric Type 5 'Deltic' in distinctive light blue, grey and cream livery awaiting departure with the 08.50 "White Rose" to Leeds on 7th July 1959. Introduced in 1955, *Deltic* was the most powerful of British diesels and which amassed more than 400,000 miles during trials whilst on loan to British Railways. The subsequent order for 22 locomotives was the beginning of one of the most successful eras of modern traction history. In contrast, some early designs were disappointing, including the 'Baby Deltics' which were born from the same EE stable. They saw an early demise under BR's plan to rationalise the diesel fleet. On the right one of the latter locomotives, No. D5906 awaits departure with a King's Cross outer surburban train.

*BR*

# DIESELS

## IN THE

# WHITE ROSE COUNTY

DAVID HEY

Oxford Publishing Co.

*Frontispiece:* Class 47 No. 47553 heads the 11.05 Liverpool-Scarborough out of Leeds in June 1983. Leeds City station was originated at the turn of the century when the North Eastern Railway extended the line from its terminus at Marsh Lane through the centre of Leeds to connect with the LNWR at Holbeck. The new line involved considerable construction work, including an embankment across the site of St Peters Parish Church graveyard (top right, lined by trees). As might have been expected there was strong public opposition to the route, and an Act of Parliament provided for the gravestones to be re-sited on the slopes of the railway embankment. The 19th Century tombstones are still visible today.

In the days before the East Coast Main Line (ECML) Selby Coalfield diversion came into operation, 'Deltic' class No. 55008 *The Green Howards* slows for the obligatory 40 mph limit over the Ouse swing bridge at Selby on 7th June 1981.The 14³/4 mile long diversion was opened on 1st October 1983, the first trains over the route being the 14.10 Newcastle-King's Cross and the 13.30 King's Cross-Newcastle – both HSTs.

A FOULIS-OPC Railway Book

**British Library Cataloguing in Publication Data**
Hey, David
Diesels in the white rose county.
1. Yorkshire. Railway services. British Rail.
Diesel locomotives, to 1988
I. Title.
625.2'66'094281

ISBN 0-86093-417-9

**Library of Congress catalog card number** 88-82512

Published by:
Haynes Publishing Group
Sparkford, Near Yeovil, Somerset. BA22 7JJ

Haynes Publications Inc.
861 Lawrence Drive, Newbury Park, California 91320, USA.

The constantly varying non-descriptive digits which appeared in headcodes was a major factor for BR's decision to dispense with headcode panels entirely. From 1976, BR decreed that operating handles were to be removed and blinds set permanently at '0000'. On occasions, vibrations caused the numbers to revolve on their own accord. Such configurations can be seen in the headcode of a Scarborough dmu (right) and celebrity locomotive No. 40145, the first of the centre-headcode Class 40s, seen beneath the classic overall roof at York. Withdrawn in May 1983, No. 40145 was destined for preservation by the Class 40 Preservation Society on the East Lancashire Light Railway, Bury.
*P. Harris*

# Introduction

Yorkshire must contain literally thousands of good railway photographic locations; from the wild sweeping moorland tops of Ribblehead to the broad acres of the South Yorkshire Coalfield. Suffice it to say that my attempt at preparing *Diesels in the White Rose County* by no means circumscribes its full potential because the abolition of the Yorkshire Ridings, together with the decimation of its many railway routes has sadly reduced the scope.

The first section of the book is devoted to the period from 1954 when diesels came to the fore. At the time, the County consisted of North, East and West Ridings, embracing a region as far north as Middlesbrough and south to Bawtry on the East Coast Main Line. The County's east-west extremity stretched from the Lancashire mill town of

Oldham, to the entire coastline from Teesside to the Humber Estuary.

For the purpose of the remainder of this book I have concentrated on the region of Yorkshire which was formed during the 1974 local Government re-organisation, when it was decreed that the Yorkshire Ridings should be abolished in favour of three new counties; North, South and West Yorkshire. Under the new county structure a large portion of the East Riding, including Goole and Hull was taken over by the new County of Humberside; a slice from the North Riding now belongs to Cleveland, and some of Yorkshire's Pennine country has been passed over to Cumbria and Lancashire. To a lesser extent the newly-formed Greater Manchester area includes a piece of the old West Riding.

Today, the railway network in the region is untidily depressing, with disused sidings, singled track and many once proud Victorian structures razed to the ground. The view is typical of latterday trends, yet it represents only a fraction of a more extensive network that was formed by competing companies eager to profit from the County's coal, steel and mineral riches. A glance at a pre-Grouping map reveals a comprehensive rail network, which at its fullest extent was anything but integrated, with many Yorkshire towns linked by duplicate routes.

In 1963 Beeching had a field day! The rationalisation of lines during that time was as indiscriminate as their construction. His plan for re-shaping British Railways had been clear enough; to make the railways pay. Yet history has revealed that it offered no solution in curing the railway's financial ills. Indeed the disturbing truth that has emerged from the carnage is that many sizeable Yorkshire towns have been removed from the railway map altogether, including Market Weighton, Ripon and Otley to name just a few.

Out of all this gloom, the rail network is now undergoing a major facelift with the opening of several new stations and the introduction of middle distance 'Sprinters' and local 'Pacer' trains in BR's programme to revamp Provincial services. Now that the first generation fleet of diesels is fast disappearing, many of the views depicted in this book are already a part of history.

The pictures are arranged in a geographical sequence from Blea Moor and Ribblehead to the low level 'carrs' around Doncaster. Individual types are highlighted on the way and it attempts to show as much as possible of the changing scene, from its origin to the present day, with photographs spanning a period from the transition from steam in the 1960s to the building of the Class 58s and second generation dmus and the new livery variations of the 1980s.

Much pleasure has been derived from my travels throughout Yorkshire, because it is an interesting place for anyone should they care to explore its vast spaces, and for those who have not already done so, then a visit to the area is highly recommended not only for its abounding variety of scenery, but for the natives' warmth of welcome.

In conclusion, my thanks go to BR, Peter Harris, Howard Malham, Ian Carr, Mike Mitchell, David Green, John Rayner, and John Wright for their help in providing photographs to fill the gaps of my own collection. Photographs are by the author unless stated otherwise.

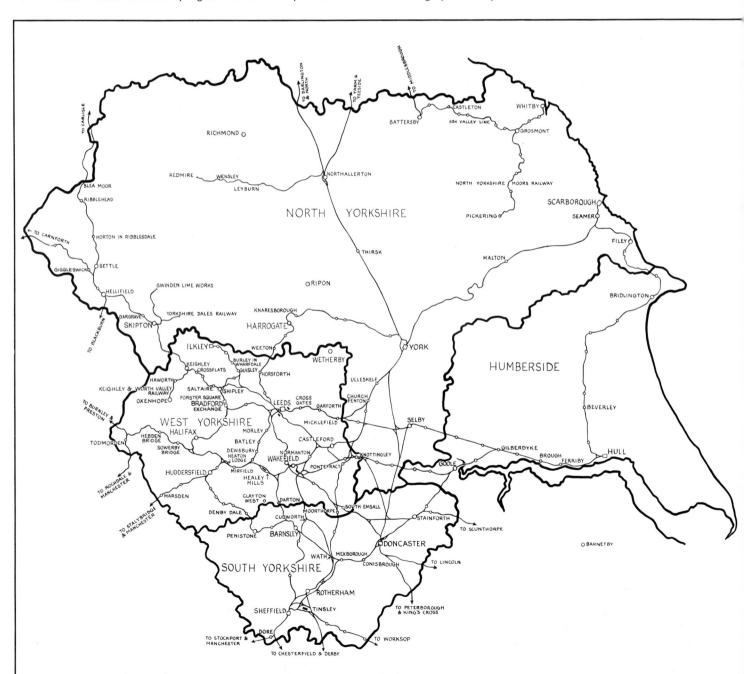

# Transition from Steam
## –
## Diesel Multiple Units

In 1954, Yorkshire became the first area to be served by dmus when the Ministry of Transport gave British Railways approval for expenditure on the introduction of a new diesel railcar service between Leeds and Bradford in the West Riding of Yorkshire. The eight 2-car vehicles were designed and built at the Derby Carriage and Wagon Works, consisting of a light alloy and steel construction, short wheelbase and low height which enabled a top speed of 62 mph and earned their name the *Derby Lightweights*. The units made their debut in April 1954, and were the true forerunners of BR's first-generation diesel railcar fleet. This BR photograph shows a brand new 2-car set composed of DMC(L) No. E79500 paired with DMB No. E79000 at Derby Works in 1954. A distinctive feature of the new railcars was their large front driving/observation windows which gave excellent visibility for passengers. *BR*

The 1955 Modernisation Plan was the beginning of a new era for Britain's railways when a fleet of nearly 5,000 diesel multiple units was introduced. It was primarily intended that they replace uneconomic steam locomotive workings on surburban and local services, cross-country and selected InterCity services throughout the rail network. Ironically, line closures outpaced their introduction, and the new dmus were not quite the saviours as hoped. In 1956, the Derby Class 114 was introduced for general branch line and local services. The fifty 2-car sets represented one of the earliest railcars of the Modernisation Plan, and carried the first numbered series 50001 – 50049 within the fleet. They were aptly named the *Derby Heavyweights*, because of their steel construction and longer underframe compared with the earlier alloy bodied Lightweights. Here, a 2-car set adorned with yellow warning flashes, white cab roof ends, and marker lights above the destination blind heads towards Leeds at Kirkstall in June 1961. In the foreground, a 'Peak' class locomotive heads the northbound "Thames Clyde Express".

*Opposite page:*
During the transition from steam, many enthusiasts never forgave BR for replacing steam-hauled branch lines with the humble dmu. Yet with the benefit of hindsight it is clear that if it were not for dmu's there would be no rural passenger network at all! Typical of the vanished scene is the Richmond branch in the North Riding which was closed to passenger traffic in March 1969. The NER terminus was situated at the end of a 9¾ mile long line which diverged from the ECML at Eryholme Junction and provided a rail connection for the military camp at Catterick. The station had an attractive roofed train shed, consisting of two 30ft spans, each of nine bays and made up of cast iron arcades with Gothic columns. Diesel multiple units were introduced on the branch in 1957 but were only able to stave off the inevitable for another twelve years. Here, an early liveried Derby Class 108 3-car set arrives on the service from Darlington in August 1961.

*Above:*
The early dmus were provided with front-end chevrons in an attempt to provide visual warning for permanent way staff. However, the 'visibility flash' or 'speed whiskers', as they were sometimes called, proved to be inadequate and they were later changed to a more conspicuous rectangular yellow warning panel. In this view a 4-car Metro-Cammell unit forming a Harrogate-Leeds Central train emerges from the cutting leading out of Bramhope Tunnel in June 1965.

*Right:*
In the opposite direction newly-painted warning panels have been applied to a 3-car Calder Valley set seen heading towards Harrogate on the same day.

At the extremity of Yorkshire's North Riding was the NER terminus at Middleton in Teesdale. The branch diverged from the Penrith-Darlington line which ran via Kirkby Stephen and Stainmore Summit across the Pennines. Passenger services were withdrawn from Fawcett Junction to Middleton in Teesdale on 30th November 1964. Here, a Birmingham Railway Carriage & Wagon Co 3-car dmu, TOPS Class 104, awaits departure on the Barnard Castle and Darlington service in July 1960. The scene is typical of a country branch line with ash trackbed, bullhead rail, cattle dock, point rodding and run-round loop – a legacy of steam days when NER A8 class 4-6-2 Tanks dominated the service.

Despite the increase in numbers of passengers and improved economies that the new dmu service brought, many closures could not be prevented and several rural passenger lines fell to the Beeching axe. One survivor is the Ilkley branch which was dieselised in 1959 and continues to provide a service for commuters to Leeds and Bradford. In this view, a 4-car Class 108 unit passes beneath Kirkstall Flyover on the Leeds-Ilkley service in May 1961. The station platforms of Armley Canal Road can be seen in the background.

Perhaps the most durable legacy of the first generation dmus is the Metropolitan-Cammell Class 101, introduced in 1956 for general branch line and local services. In this view, a 2-car set forming the Saturday 12.40 Harrogate-Leeds City is seen between Spofforth and Wetherby West Junction on 22nd December 1962. The service between Leeds to Wetherby and Harrogate, and Wetherby to Church Fenton was withdrawn on 6th January 1964 involving closure of eleven intermediate stations. It was the first passenger service in Yorkshire to fall victim to the re-shaping report published the previous year. *M. Mitchell*

The 'Blue Square' code system was one of five basic coupling systems introduced from 1955, to provide operating flexibility between the various types of power cars and trailers making up the first generation classes of dmus. The units equipped with the blue square code have standard transmission which enables them to work in multiple and provides a convenient solution for the operating department when additional passenger accommodation is required. With the blue square symbols visible above the buffers, a mixed combination of Derby and Metro-Cammell twin-sets, make up a Harrogate-Leeds train near Wortley Junction. The viaduct in the background carries the Harrogate line across the river Aire and the Leeds-Liverpool Canal at Kirkstall.

In 1964, BR's operating fleet entered the much maligned era of blue and yellow anonymity when the Corporate Identity Programme was introduced. During the livery change period, a 3-car 'Calder Valley' set made up of green and blue vehicles, both with full yellow ends, leaves Normanton for York on 1st August 1967. In the right background, a WD 2-8-0 shunts wagons in the yard.

*M. Mitchell*

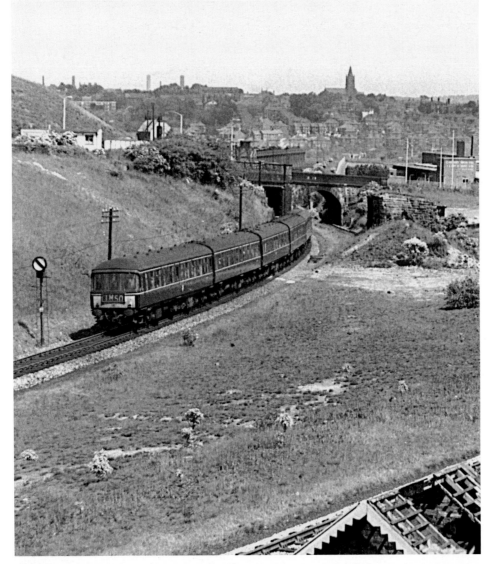

The subject of Yorkshire dmus would not be complete without the inclusion of the Trans-Pennine InterCity units. Introduced in 1960, the Swindon built 6-car sets consisted of four powered vehicles which gave an engine horsepower of 1,840 for the difficult Trans-Pennine route. The power-weight ratio made possible substantial acceleration over the gradients and provided a total running time of 163 minutes for the 128 mile route between Hull and Liverpool. With the Griddle car now removed, a 5-car set runs downhill to Farnley Junction on the Liverpool-Hull service in August 1964. The ex-LNWR steam shed (55C) can be seen above the bridge in the background.

In 1959, the British Transport Commission announced the basis of its £1,240 million Modernisation Plan for the country's railways. It involved the delivery of several pilot scheme main line locomotives so that operating experience with various manufacturers' equipment could be evaluated under service conditions. The Eastern Region took delivery of ten pilot scheme English Electric Type 4s, with Nos D200, D202-D205 going to Stratford, and Nos D201, D206-D209 to Hornsey for the GN line out of King's Cross. At the beginning of the winter timetable, the ER revived the GN Sheffield route with the introduction of a new diesel hauled Pullman service between King's Cross and Sheffield Victoria. The lightweight Pullman ran twice each way daily; the first 'up' morning and 'down' evening trips being given the title "Master Cutler", while the slower midday runs included stops at Peterborough, Grantham and Retford and were not named. This BR publicity-posed photograph shows No. D207 with "Master Cutler" headboard on 29th September 1961. A typical diagram for the Hornsey Type 4s was the 'down' "Master Cutler" out of King's Cross and the next morning's 07.20 return from Sheffield Victoria, spending their time in the Yorkshire area with overnight freight workings to and from Annesley Yard, Nottingham. *BR*

The pedigree of the Class 55s stretches back to the days before the announcement of the pilot scheme orders when the English Electric Co. had already completed the prototype *Deltic* at their own expense. *(See page four.)* Introduced in 1955, the locomotive ran trials on the London Midland Region before being transferred to the ER out of King's Cross. Its performance on the GN line was soon appreciated and an order for 22 locomotives was placed in 1958 to replace 55 Pacifics on the East Coast route. The first production 'Deltic' was delivered to Finsbury Park in March 1961. In this view, No. D9010 *The King's Own Scottish Borderer* heads the Bradford portion of the "White Rose Pullman" towards Exchange station in October 1965. *H. Malham*

Darlington built Class 24 No. D5099 heads the Harrogate portion of the 13.20 King's Cross-Leeds-Harrogate towards Weeton on 17th May 1964. This class first appeared in 1958 when a batch of 20 pilot scheme locomotives was built at Derby. The Type 2 Bo-Bos of Class 24 performed well until the late 1970s when they were withdrawn as surplus to the requirements of the day.                                                                                         *M. Mitchell*

One of the most successful of the pilot scheme designs was the 'Peaks'. Originally designated of Type 4 classification, later to become known as Classes 44, 45 and 46. The ten pilot scheme Class 44 s were equipped with 2,300bhp engines, whereas the Class 45 and 46 locomotives were powered by Sulzer engines of 2,500bhp, giving a maximum tractive effort of 55,000lb. The three classes shared the same bodyshell and were basically similar in appearance, except that the 46s were fitted with a centrally placed headcode panel and internally they were provided with Brush electrical equipment instead of Crompton Parkinson. The 'Peaks' were introduced on the Newcastle-Liverpool service in 1963. Here, Class 46 No. D190 (later 46053) heads the 15.16 to Liverpool on the steeply-graded Wetherby route between Bardsey and Thorner on 6th June 1963.                                                                                         *M. Mitchell*

# Type 4s

In 1957, the British Transport Commission defined a Type 4 locomotive as having between 2,000 and 2,750 engine horsepower. The most successful of these has been the Brush/Sulzer Co-Cos, later Class 47 which represent the most numerous main line diesel class in operation on BR. Here, No. D1571 (later 47545) heads the southbound "Yorkshire Pullman" past Beeston Junction in May 1965. The titled train was withdrawn in May 1978, to be re-instated seven years later with the introduction of a new Pullman service made up of a refurbished HST. The train began operations on the 07.30 Leeds-King's Cross and the 17.55 return to Leeds and Bradford in May 1985.

'Peak' class No. D147 (later 46010) heads the northbound "Thames Clyde Express" through Newlay Cutting on the outskirts of Leeds in August 1965. The "Thames Clyde" was inaugurated in 1927 between St Pancras and Glasgow, but lost its title at the end of the 1974/75 timetable. All through workings between London and Glasgow via the Midland Main Line ceased two years later, and the service is now maintained by the Nottingham-Glasgow trains via Manchester and the West Coast Main Line.

During the transition from steam, the early diesels shared stabling facilities at steam sheds. The allocation of the 'Peaks' to Holbeck shed commenced in March 1961, and from the start of the summer timetable the "Thames Clyde" and "Waverley" expresses became diesel hauled throughout. Despite the filth and grime of such conditions, the smart livery of the 'Peaks' with their grey roof, side grilles and body band still contrasted well with the standard locomotive green. Here, No. D50 (later 45040) heads a uniform rake of maroon Mk1 coaching stock through Newlay Cutting in June 1964. The locomotive was named *King's Shropshire Light Infantry* in May the following year.

At 2,000hp, the EE Co. Type 4s just qualified for the Type 4 category, but as loads increased they were found to be underpowered for the fast ECML expresses. Displaced by the more powerful 47s and 'Deltics', the Class 40s found regular duties on the cross-country service between Merseyside and the North East. Here, No. D270 heads the 15.16 Newcastle-Liverpool on the 3½ mile long climb at 1 in 70 to Gildersome Tunnel on 1st August 1964. The line was built by the LNWR as an alternative route between Huddersfield and Leeds via the Spen Valley. Local passenger services were withdrawn in 1953, but the line remained open for the through Trans-Pennine service until 1965.

*M. Mitchell*

# Train Identification

*Above and right:*
When the four-character headcode displays were devised for main line diesels, it was relatively simple to identify trains being worked. The first numeral identified the class of train, followed by a letter indicating the destination, whilst the next two digits represented the train reporting number. In this view *(above)* the roller blind of Class 46 No. D157 (later 46020) shows 2N71 on the 12.30 Morecambe-Leeds, seen crossing the River at Kirkstall on 28th May 1963. *Right,* the divided headcode boxes of Class 45 No. D72 (later 45050) display 1S 68, the "Thames Clyde Express" as it heads north through Newlay & Horsforth on 5th July 1963.

The Class 40s sported three variations in their front ends, the first 125 locomotives were built with a disc headcode system, followed by 20 locomotives with split headcode boxes either side of the nose. The remainder of the class appeared with a much neater centrally positioned headcode panel. The disc-type headcode display was a direct inheritance of the steam era. Here, No. D241 assists B1 class 4-6-0 No. 61030 *Nyala* on Micklefield Bank with the Heaton-Manchester (Red Bank) empty vans on 2nd April 1961. The combination of opened discs reveal a locomotive headlamp code for a goods train composed of not less than one third vacuum-braked stock with brake pipe connected to the engine.

*M. Mitchell*

The first 20 Brush A1A-A1A Type 2s, or Class 31/0 as they became known, were built with headcode marker discs. (Warning horns were mounted in the roof-end grille). With the introduction of the four-character identification system, later constructions had roof-mounted headcode boxes as standard, but due to supply difficulties the modification was not adopted fully until No. 31143 in the series. Class 31/1 No. 31102 was one to receive headcode discs, two of which have since been removed when photographed at Holbeck on 24th May, 1981. The discs were hinged centrally which exposed marker lights for night time identification; in this case, an express passenger headlamp code, but this is most unlikely for a 'Skinhead' Class 31/1!

# Type 3s

Introduced in 1960, the English Electric 1,750hp Co-Co Type 3s quickly established their outstanding versatility on passenger and freight work. The EE Co. (now GEC Traction Ltd) were able to make rapid deliveries due to their consecutive construction at the company's Vulcan Foundry, Newton-le-Willows and Stephenson Works, Darlington. No. D6737 (later 37037) was built in the first batch of 69 locomotives to be delivered from the Vulcan Foundry. It is seen heading an 'up' Ford train made up of old car-carrying bogie wagons and the newer 'Cartic' two tier vehicles on 19th March 1966. The ensemble was photographed between Hampole and Carcroft on the former GN line between Leeds and Doncaster.

*M. Mitchell*

During the 1960s Class 40s, 37s and 25s were coupled to brake tenders to provide sufficient brake power for non-fitted and partially fitted goods trains. The tenders were equivalent to six brake wagons and were of low profile so as not to obstruct the driver's forward vision. Here, Type 3 Co-Co No. D6770 (later 37070) propels a diesel brake tender downgrade near Thorner with a rake of empty bolsters in November 1962.

*M. Mitchell*

# Type 2s

Under the 1955 Modernisation Plan pilot scheme it was decreed that diesel locomotives of between 1,000 and 1,365 engine horsepower would be classified as Type 2s. The most numerous were the BR/Sulzer Bo-Bo Class 25s which were evolved from the first 151 locomotives of TOPS Class 24. During the course of construction, several body design changes were made, including the re-siting of engine room ventilation louvres at cant rail height. The filthy condition of No. D5176, (later TOPS Class 25/1 25026), shows the cluttered bodyside position of the air intake grilles as the Type 2 heads ecs from Harrogate to Leeds.

The first order for the production Brush Type 2 A1A-A1As was made in 1958. They were built to the same basic design as the 20 pilot scheme locomotives still under construction at Loughbrough, except that the Mirrlees engine was uprated to a new standard setting of 1,365hp. It was later found that the engines showed a pronounced tendency to fail from fatigue and a re-engining programme of the whole fleet was carried out using English Electric engines of 1,470hp. In all, a total of 243 locomotives were built. Here, No D5844 heads a Class 7 freight near Crigglestone on 7th August 1967.          *M. Mitchell*

## Type 1s

Although less glamorous that its larger EE Co. relatives, the 1,000hp Bo-Bo Type 1, (TOPS Class 20), is perhaps one of the most successful diesel classes to emerge from BR's modernisation programme. Introduced in 1957, they became the first type of locomotive delivered under the 1955 pilot scheme orders. Today, they are the only Type 1 still going strong. Here, pilot scheme veteran No. 20010 is accompanied by Class 37 No. 37226 at Wath depot on 27th June 1981. During the early 1960s, BR had a predominance of locomotives in the 1,000/1,250hp range and relatively few in the 2,000/2,500hp group. As a result, the Class 20s were working in multiple almost from new. Although the cab ends were officially regarded as the rear, the practice of working nose-to-nose was adopted early on due to the improved visibility preferred by drivers. Below: Class 20s Nos 20066 and 20095 head a train of redundant track for Healey Mills past Cudworth South Junction in April 1982.

The transition from steam brought with it a new diesel dialogue and familiar prose like 'Crabs', 'Lizzies', 'Semi's', 'Streaks' etc was soon replaced by a new choice of language:- 'Whistlers' 'Hoovers', 'Choppers', and 'Duffs' – to name just a few. 'Double Headers', operated by one driver became known as 'Multiple working', whereas coupled locomotives driven independently were called 'Tandem workings'. Neither is the case here as Standard Class 4 4-6-0 No. 75059 is required to provide front-end assistance for ailing 'Rat' Type 2 No. D7589 on the 2N71 Morecambe-Leeds at Hirst Wood Sidings near Bingley on 5th March 1965. BR usually avoided such combinations owing to the risk of hot ashes dropping from the leading steam locomotive which could ignite the accumulative oil deposits on the underside of the trailing diesel. Consequently, when the operating department was required to provide double-headed steam/diesel combinations, it was obligatory for the steam locomotive to be coupled inside. A more conventional pairing is therefore seen below with Class 25 No. D5175 piloting an unidentified Class 9F 2-10-0 on a Heysham-Hunslet tank train at Skipton North Junction in September 1967.

*Both: H. Malham*

## Double Headers

# North Yorkshire

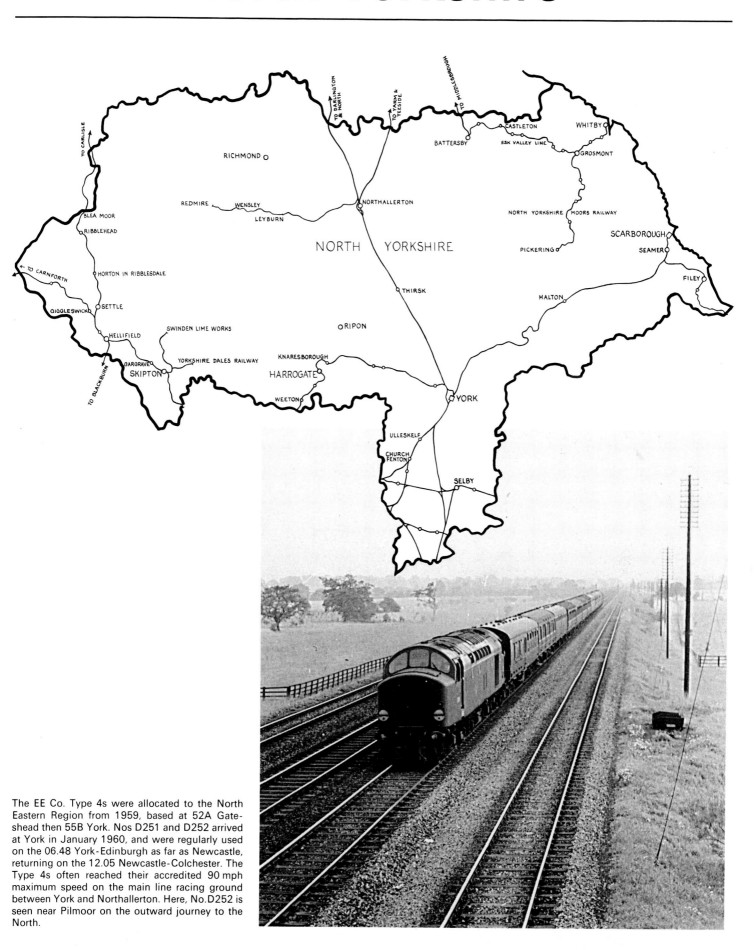

The EE Co. Type 4s were allocated to the North Eastern Region from 1959, based at 52A Gateshead then 55B York. Nos D251 and D252 arrived at York in January 1960, and were regularly used on the 06.48 York-Edinburgh as far as Newcastle, returning on the 12.05 Newcastle-Colchester. The Type 4s often reached their accredited 90 mph maximum speed on the main line racing ground between York and Northallerton. Here, No.D252 is seen near Pilmoor on the outward journey to the North.

# North Yorkshire

If you wish to discover the green and pleasant land that is England, you should spend some time exploring North Yorkshire. It is geographically the largest county in England, stretching from the Yorkshire Dales National Park in the west, across the Vale of York, to the North Yorkshire Moors and holiday resorts of Scarborough and Whitby on the east coast.

North Yorkshire is almost wholly agricultural and the development of its railways consisted of many rural branch lines that carried goods and mineral traffic. Local passenger services were infrequently used; doubtless due to the distances of some stations from the villages they served. The remoteness of Dent station on the magnificent Settle-Carlisle line is perhaps an extreme example, being a full four miles from the community and situated at 1,145ft above sea level.

The rail network in the region began with the opening of a primitive horse drawn tramway between Whitby and Pickering. Today, the tunnel at Grosmont on the original line provides access for visitors to the running and repair shops of the North Yorkshire Moors Railway which operates a well-balanced fleet of steam and diesel traction over the picturesque 18 mile route between Pickering and Grosmont.

Elsewhere in the region there is much to interest the enthusiast; from the bleak moorland surroundings of the Esk Valley line to the superb scenery of the Settle-Carlisle route. The proposal for closure of the S&C has aroused much interest and support in recent years. At the start of the 1987 summer timetable, a local authority-supported service was introduced calling at eight re-opened stations, 17 years after BR had axed the service. But to what extent the increase in S&C traffic owes its origin to the threat of closure can only be determined as time goes by. It is hoped that 'England's greatest historical route' will last forever.

York is the main railway centre in the region, perhaps most famed for its museums, particularly the National Railway Museum which was established in the former steam shed roundhouse in 1967. Visitors are able to reflect on the history of Britain's railways portrayed by rolling stock and relics of the past, including several diesels withdrawn from service in more recent years.

Despite several flaws which manifested themselves during early service, the Type 4 (Class 40) eventually became established as the standard locomotive for ECML express working. No.D246 is seen heading south through the now closed Temple Hirst station on the former ECML near Selby. The early Type 4s were fitted with a nose front ladder, used by servicing staff to gain access to two hinged hatches on top of the nose.

The Class 56s are the unsung heroes of BR as they haul the endless procession of merry-go-round trains from pit to power station. Heading past the now demolished Higham Crossing Box between Monk Fryston and Knottingley, Romanian built 56 No. 56021 hauls mgr empties for the South Yorkshire Coalfield in June 1981.

Class 31/4 No. 31411 heads the 16.10 Carlisle-Leeds through Hellifield South Junction on 8th July 1983. In the background, Class 40 No. 40004 awaits the arrival of train crew men from Skipton to collect the 6E32 21.19 Clitheroe-Middlesbrough cement train, due to locomotive failure on the 6M69 empties from Middlesbrough.

## Blea Moor – Settle

For many years the future of the Settle-Carlisle line has been in some doubt. Its decline as a major rail artery culminated with the re-routing of the scheduled Nottingham-Glasgow expresses via the Hope Valley line which clearly revealed BR's intention to demise the S&C. But it was not until August 1983 that the rumour for closure was confirmed. By then, only a modicum of freight, together with two daily passenger services in each direction formed the line's regular service. The announcement saw the beginning of the longest public hearing ever held by the Transport Users Consultative Committee. Southbound passenger trains enter North Yorkshire proper from Blea Moor Tunnel. Here, a Class 31 heads the 16.35 Carlisle-Leeds past Blea Moor Sidings in July 1983.

The S&C can boast some of the most spectacular railway engineering to be found in England. Easily the most impressive structure on the 72 mile route is the quarter mile long viaduct at Ribblehead. It stands 165ft high above the valley on 24 magnificent spans and looks massive in its barren surroundings. The blunt disclosure by BR of the deterioration of the viaduct and the cost of repair was one of the main reasons for their decision to close the line. The lofty structure dominates the view as a Class 47 leaves a trail of exhaust while accelerating the 16.10 Leeds-Carlisle from the 30 mph limit imposed on the viaduct.

BR civil engineers stated that the deterioration of the stonework of Ribblehead Viaduct was due to the collapse of the waterproof membrane which had allowed more than a century of Pennine weather to erode the piers. To alleviate further stress cracking the stonework, the double track was reduced to a single, centrally positioned line. The work was coincident with track layout alterations at Blea Moor involving the removal of the 'down' siding and goods loop, whilst the accompanying semaphores were replaced by single and multi-aspect colour light signals. In the days before rationalisation was carried out, Class 25/2 No. 25207 heads the lightweight 16.10 Leeds-Carlisle across the double track viaduct in September 1983.

The S&C runs through the celebrated 'Three Peaks' countryside of Whernside, Ingleborough and Penyghent which looms on the horizon like a crouching lion with the top of the fell – 'hill of the winds' across the summit. Class 25 No. 25322 clatters downhill towards Horton in Ribblesdale with the 10.22 7E54 Ribblehead-Healey Mills stone train in July 1983.

Ironically, on the very day that the S&C closure notice was published, the WCML overhead wires were down at Lancaster and trains were diverted via the S&C whilst repairs were carried out. It clearly illustrates what an indispensible asset the line is as a diversionary route when such trouble occurs. Over 40 trains were diverted, including this one, headed by a Class 47 near Sheriff Brow. On the left can be seen the 1,748yd long viaduct which carries the line 55ft above the River Ribble. The structure is built on the skew with heavy wing retaining walls.

The Midland Railway architecture to be found on the S&C is of Gothic style which gives the buildings the ruggedness of ancient manor houses. Here, the steeply pitched roofs at Horton in Ribblesdale station hasten away a sudden downpour as Class 31/4 No. 31404, customised with white body stripe, heads the 16.10 Carlisle-Leeds on 1st July 1983. The lines on the left lead to Delanys stone sidings.

Following the withdrawal of Nottingham-Glasgow expresses via the S&C in 1981, passengers from West Yorkshire found only a minimum service to Carlisle and west Scotland. The inadequacies of the trains attracted unfavourable attention and BR introduced the elderly Trans-Pennine sets to provide a fast connecting service for the north via the WCML at Lancaster. Here, the 10.35 Leeds-Morecambe accelerates from Settle Junction in August 1983. The 'Long Drag' starts proper here and climbs for 20 miles to 1,169ft above sea level at Ais Gill Summit.

# Hellifield – Skipton

Once an important railway centre, the MR station at Hellifield stands as a monument to a bygone age when it provided connections from Lancashire and the West Riding to Scotland. Local passenger services were withdrawn from the ex LYR Blackburn line in 1962 and the steam shed closed a year later. Diverted from the WCML on Sunday 20th November 1983, Class 47 No. 47588 cautiously negotiates Hellifield South Junction to gain the Blackburn line with the 07.23 Glasgow-Birmingham New Street. Hellifield station is listed as a building of architectural and historical interest, but the deteriorating structure is untidily depressing, and BR are seeking to demolish part of the wrought iron canopy to reduce maintenance costs.

The raking light shows that the unofficial *Warrior* name has been removed from the bodyside of veteran Class 40 No. 40104 as it heads the 6M37 Haverton Hill-Moss Sidings ICI tanks out of the goods loop at Skipton. The severed track in the foreground once formed Skipton North Junction where the MR line diverged to Colne. Passenger services were withdrawn in February 1970 and the track was lifted soon after.

With the MR insignia and ornate iron supports visible in the background, Class 31/4 No. 31446 restarts the 15.50 Hull-Lancaster on a very wet 2nd October 1984. The withdrawal of the Trans-Pennine units saw the re-instatement of a loco-hauled service at the start of the 1984 summer timetable.

The complexity of present day railway operation can be found at Skipton which lies within the London Midland Region administered from Preston, yet the majority of its passenger rail services are sponsored by the WPTA's 'Airedale' service from Leeds, and cross-country Leeds-Morecambe trains come under the auspices of the Eastern Region. The anomaly may be short-lived however, following the revival of the Copy Pit line and the many sizeable towns along its route which offers a more lucrative connection between West Yorkshire and Lancashire. Quarrying adds much to the prosperity of Skipton's rail traffic. Here, white roofed Class 47 No. 47114 sorts out a ballast train in March 1985.

## Grassington Branch

Skipton in Craven, to give it its local title, was first reached by the MR via the Aire Valley from Leeds in 1847. The Ilkley line was opened 40 years later which gave an alternative route to Leeds via the Wharfe Valley, up to closure in March 1965. In this view, Class 31s Nos 31203 and 31343 head past the derelict Ilkley platforms with the 10.18 Rylstone-Dairycoates Tilcon train in September 1983. The train will reverse in Broughton Yard before continuing the journey to Hull via Leeds. In the background, a Leeds-Lancaster Trans-Pennine set stands at the main running platforms, while the centre platform loop is occupied by a 2-car dmu.

Class 31s pass the MR junction at Embsay with the Tilcon train for Hull. Contrary to appearances, the former MR line to Ilkley (right background) is isolated from BR metals at this point, and the Yorkshire Dales Railway Society is confined to a stretch of track based at Embsay station. The Society was launched with the intention of using the old line from Skipton to Grassington as a steam tourist railway, but later turned its attention instead to re-open the branch to Bolton Abbey on the former MR route to Ilkley.

31

*Left:* A general view of Tilcon Swinden Limeworks near Cracoe on the former Grassington branch which was opened in 1902 under the title of the Yorkshire Dales Railway. The Company originally intended to construct a line that would join the MR in the Skipton area to the NE main line south of Darlington, but when the Government refused the Bill a less ambitious line terminating at Grassington was built instead. Today, much of the line remains open for lime traffic from the Tilcon quarry near Cracoe. In this view, the area is shrouded in a liberal coating of dust as the Tilcon wagons are hauled through the rapid loading plant by one of the company's shunters. The pair of Class 31s in the foreground are led by No. 31128.

# Harrogate Line

How the venerable EE Type 4s will be remembered is epitomized in this view of No. D234 heading an almost uniform rake of BR standard Mk1 stock on an inter-regional train during the 1960s. This heavy, twelve coach train is the 11.00 Liverpool-Newcastle seen near Weeton on 1st August 1960. The rapid decline in the ranks of steam saw the Class 40s take over many InterCity expresses on the ER and LMR. During steam days, the Liverpool-Newcastle expresses were usually double-headed by a pair of 6Ps, 'Jubilees' or 'Patriots' over the Stanhedge route, whilst a standard 2-6-4T assisted an A3 Pacific over the steeply graded line from Leeds to Harrogate. The Class 40s performed the task single-handed throughout. *M. Mitchell*

A location very popular with aspiring freelancers of the steam hauled "Scarborough Spa Express" is Wescoe Hill Tunnel near Weeton. In this view, BR/Sulzer Type 2 No. D5178 heads an interesting collection of old stock forming the 11.25 SO Newcastle-Llandudno on 7th July 1965. The quantity production of the Type 2s, later to become Class 25s produced many changes during construction before a fully satisfactory design was evolved. It led to a wide detail variation for what was intended to be a standard class. This Darlington-built Type 2 was one of a batch uprated to 1,250hp, but retaining a bodystyle similar to the original Class 24s from which the 25s were a development. *M. Mitchell*

The 138 year old viaduct at Knaresborough is regularly featured on BR posters to lure travellers to the region. The 300ft long viaduct has four arches which carry the Harrogate-York line 90 feet above the Nidd Gorge. The foundation stone was laid in April 1846, but as the work was nearing completion, on 11th March 1848, the whole mass of stonework collapsed into the river below. The viaduct was rebuilt in a more substantial manner, including turreted piers which blend in with the picturesque town. Here, a Class 141 railbus slows for the Knaresborough stop on the Leeds-York service in April 1985. Note the ornate signal cabin at the end of the station platforms on the right.

Following the completion of four tracks on the ECML between York and Northallerton, serious doubts were raised about the future of the Ripon line as a through route when the majority of trains which previously used the line were re-routed via York. In 1967, all trains between Harrogate and Northallerton were withdrawn and the track lifted soon after. Here, Class 40 No. D284 heads the 11.10 Newcastle-Liverpool over the River Ure at Ripon on 3rd April 1965. With the continuing decline of the railway network, the heyday of Ripon's station and, for that matter the Class 40s, are now but just a memory. *H. Malham*

## Early Diesels –

## East Coast Main Line

Brush Type 4 Co-Co No. D1676 (later 47090) *Vulcan* heads the 13.00 Newcastle-King's Cross over Wiske Moor troughs, just north of Northallerton. This was one of 17 locomotives, Nos D1660-D1676 allocated to the Western Region which were named during 1965/66. *Vulcan* is perhaps one of the most popular of all locomotive names. Numerous locomotives have carried *Vulcan* nameplates, ranging from an 0-6-0 saddle tank, GWR 'Bulldog' class 4-4-0; LNWR 'Precedent' 2-4-0 and 'Prince of Wales' 4-6-0, LMS 'Royal Scot', BR 'Britannia' Class 4-6-2 and the WD 2-8-0 No. 90732, one of the last engines built to Ministry of Supply design and purchased by British Railways in 1948. More recently the name was applied to Class 45 No. 45106, one of the last survivors of this once extensive class. *Ian S. Carr*

'Deltic' No. D9005 *The Prince of Wales's Own Regiment of Yorkshire* heads the 10.10 King's Cross-Edinburgh over Wiske Moor troughs on 19th July 1969. In the days before electrical train heating was introduced, water troughs were retained on some long distance routes so that diesels could replenish water supply for steam heating boilers. Diesels were equipped with a scoop which worked on the same principle as those fitted to the tenders of steam locomotives. The fleet of 22 locomotives in the 'Deltic' class were not eth fitted until 1971. Note the concrete slabs on each side of the 'Fast' lines which protect the ballast from water erosion. *Ian S. Carr*

With the speed restriction 'C' for commence for 'up' trains visible on the left, Class 46 No. D184 (later 46047) accelerates a northbound train between York and Northallerton on 10th April 1965. The locomotive was one of a batch (Nos D166-D193) allocated to Gateshead for ECML expresses and the North East-South West services. The Class 46s were rendered non-standard during the late 1970's, and in 1980 the process of running-down had already begun when several locomotives were stored at Swindon surplus to requirements. By 1984, the 56 members of the class had been withdrawn entirely.

*M. Mitchell*

Following BR's re-numbering of its diesel fleet, the EE Co. Type 3s became known as Class 37. With the 'D' prefix removed, No. 6705 (later 37005) heads northbound empties through Northallerton in May 1974. Although many of BR's aged classes of diesel have been phased out, it is expected that the 37s will be in front line duty for many years, particularly on the ER which has the largest allocation of the fleet.

*J. Rayner*

The ECML runs on straight and level ground enabling high speed performances on the IC125 service north of York. The line was used as proving ground for the prototype HST which achieved a world record of 143 mph during trials. Regaining speed from an engineering slack, 'Deltic' class No. 55017 *The Durham Light Infantry* heads the 07.15 Plymouth-Edinburgh through Northallerton in August 1981.

During the early thirties, widening of the ECML to four tracks involved a burrowing connection at Northallerton to segregate the increased Teesside traffic from the premier Anglo-Scottish expresses. Whilst A167 road traffic builds up, Class 40 No. 40158 heads past Low Gates Crossing with empty bogies from Teesside.

Although passenger traffic was withdrawn from Wensleydale branch in 1954, there is no mistaking its North Eastern Railway origin as Class 47 No. 47231 heads the daily 08.45 Redmire-Redcar mineral train through Wensley (Above) and Leyburn station (Below) on 22nd May 1983. The Wensleydale branch once formed a through route from the MR at Garsdale to the NER at Northallerton. Goods traffic was almost wholly agricultural and in particular dairy produce, but early in the century quarries were opened at Leyburn and Redmire, and it is traffic from the Tilcon quarry at Redmire which now keeps the line open.

## Branch Lines

The Beeching Report, published in 1963, proposed closure of the picturesque Esk Valley line, but it was reprieved when the Government decided that the route provided a vital link for the isolated villages in some of the remotest parts of the North Yorkshire Moors. In this view, NER detail can still be found at Battersby Junction as a Middlesbrough-Whitby dmu heads towards the Esk Valley in June 1983. On the left is a standard pattern water crane which has an extended arm to reach engines standing on both platform roads. The line ceased to be a through route when the section to Picton was closed in 1954, and trains now have to reverse at Battersby, exchanging single line tokens for the Whitby and Middlesbrough sections.

Situated in the heart of some veritable North Yorkshire countryside is Castleton station, once the terminus of the line from Picton on the Yarm-Northallerton route before the NER completed the section to Grosmont. The station was re-named Castleton Moor in 1965 and it has retained much of its charm – although the surviving notice offers contemptuous odds for drivers on the derelict coal staithes! A Whitby-Middlesbrough dmu approaches the station in July 1983.

The coastal resort of Whitby lies in a sheltered position at the mouth of the River Esk. Of the four routes that converged on the town only the Esk Valley line survives. The Whitby-Loftus line was closed in 1958, followed seven years later by the withdrawal of the scenic coastal route to Scarborough and the line to York via Pickering. In this view, a 3-car Metro-Cammell unit heads out from Whitby on the Esk Valley line in July 1983. On the right can be seen the former steam shed which closed in 1959 sending its allocation of five engines to York, Low Moor and Neville Hill, just one year after dmu operations began.

The Esk Valley line is an outstanding scenic railway, but the cost of operating the line is substantial. Unmanned stations have contributed to savings, while the recent 'Eskplore' campaign has seen additional passenger traffic over the route. In 1973, the opening of the NYMR with its BR rail connection at Grosmont, has provided the best revenue earning potential. On 1st October 1983, re-instated Class 40 No. 40122 runs alongside the Esk out of Whitby with the return leg of the F&W Railtour's "Moors Marauder". The tour coincided with the NYMR's Diesel Day when preserved diesels operated the line's passenger service between Pickering and Grosmont.

# NYMR

The NYMR is host to several diesels – the first one being Class 24 No. D5032 which arrived on the line following a request by the Forestry Commission for a cessation of steam working during the hot dry summer of 1976. The fire risk within the National Park is always a problem, and the introduction of a well balanced steam/diesel fleet has offered a permanent solution to the hazard of steam operation through the coniferous forests.

*Right:* With the usual compliment of 'haulage enthusiasts' in the leading coach, Beyer-Peacock 'Hymek' no. D7029 heads the 12.55 ex-Grosmont towards Goathland.

*Below:* The tabular hills of the North Yorkshire Moors with their distinctive heather clad plateaux can be clearly seen as D5032 runs downhill through Newtondale.

*Above:* The NYMR became home to the Deltic Preservation Society's Nos 55009 and 55019 which arrived from Doncaster in August 1982. Here, No. 55019 *Royal Highland Fusilier* heads the 12.20 from Pickering on the final stages of the climb to Goathland.

*No. 31 Meteor* 0-6-0T (Stephenson & Hawthorns 7604 of 1956) makes a dramatic exit from Grosmont on the climb to Goathland. On the right stands the Drewry Class 04 Shunter No. D2207, acquired for preservation in 1973.

# Scarborough – York

*Above:*

The popularity of Scarborough as a holiday resort is largely due to the enterprise of the NER. At the turn of the century, the Spa town thrived as NER excursions brought thousands of holidaymakers to the resort. Framed by the now demolished signal gantry, Class 47 No. 47501 heads the 14.05 to York on 31st May 1983. In the background, Class 45 No. 45004 *Irish Fusilier* waits with a returning special to Bradford, whilst Class 31 No. 31126 provides the motive power for a return excursion to Sheffield. In September 1984, BR engineers rationalised trackwork at Scarborough, reducing the station to five platforms and concentrating all signalling on Falsgrave box.

*Middle:*

An idle moment between trains provides this impromptu shot of York's Class 03 shunter appearing to be breaking all records at Scarborough. The 'panning' technique gives the illusion of great speed, when in fact No. 03073 passed the camera at less than walking pace returning ECS to the platform. Introduced in 1957, the 204hp 0-6-0 diesel mechanical shunters, total built 230, were a useful addition to the BR fleet, but by the time this photograph was taken there were only a few remaining in BR ownership. Many of the redundant Class 03s have found their way into private industry, while several more have been acquired by preservation societies for shunting duties.

*Right:*

The NER was well known for stations with overall roofs, only a few of which survive today. The almost mindless excesses of the Beeching era has seen wholesale destruction on a massive scale. Fortunately, 'Listed Building Status' has prevented many historical buildings being torn down, yet BR continue to seek ways to reduce their maintenance bill, including the demolition of the attractive station roof at Filey which was considered unsafe and beyond economic repair. Here, the 12.25 Scarborough-Hull arrives at Filey on 1st September 1983.

During the night of 20th May 1983, torrential rainfall caused a landslip on the York-Scarborough line near Kirkham Abbey. Several days of single line working was introduced, followed by a 10 mph restriction for York bound trains. Here, the Kirkham Abbey signalman returns to the box having cautioned the driver of No. 47501 on the 14.25 Scarborough-Liverpool on 31st May. The station at Kirkham closed to passengers in 1930.

# York

'Deltic' devotees will tell you that the withdrawal of the 22 locomotives happened all too quickly. Like the 'Westerns' and 'Warships' before them, the 'Deltics' were to attract an enormous following which reached almost epidemic proportions during their final years! On this occasion, no less than a dozen photographers assembled on the road overbridge at Clifton to photograph the smoky exit of No. 55017 *The Durham Light Infantry* with the 07.05 Plymouth-Edinburgh – a regular turn for the 'Deltics' to haul a service passenger train out of King's Cross on 31st December 1981.

A bitter and cold York station echoes to the familiar sound of twin Napier engines as No. 55022 *Royal Scots Grey* heads the 10.47 York-King's Cross semi-fast. Those mourning the demise of the 'Deltics' are reconciled with the thought that several members of the class have been saved from the cutter's torch, this one included, but it had to wait a while. Rejected by the Deltic Preservation Society in favour of Nos 55009 and 55019, the locomotive was to find a saviour with the D9000 Locomotive Group and preservation on the Nene Valley Railway.

York Minster is the fifth ecclesiastical building on the site which dominates any view of the city. The tower looms on the horizon as Class 40 and 31 repose at York depot in June 1982. York shed closed in 1967 and the roundhouse building was renovated to become the home of the National Railway Museum where preserved steam and diesel locomotives can be found grouped round the turntable. However, no such fate awaited Class 40 No. 40025 *Lusitania,* for although some Class 40s survived a while longer within BR's Departmental fleet, No. 40025 was withdrawn from traffic at Healey Mills in October 1982.

York station is one of the largest and busiest on BR, served by 53 IC125s every weekday and dealing with more than 5 million passengers a year. The station has a grandeur and style befitting a great railway centre, consisting of an arched roof curved from end to end and made up of four semi-circular arches with a centre span 81ft high. The great roof reverberates with the whistle of Class 40 No. 40007, one of the Eastern Region stalwarts of 1958, heading a Scarborough train on 19th June 1976.

*P. Harris*

Following the introduction of full IC125 service on the ECML the diesel running shed at York was closed to all but minor maintenance, at the end of 1981. Earlier in the year, 'Deltic' class No. 55012 *Crepello* stands in York depot on 7th June. The locomotive retains the white window surround which adorned the Finsbury Park 'Deltics' transferred to York when the FP main line diesel depot ceased operations. *Crepello* was withdrawn from service on 18th May, taken to York for removal of some parts, then towed to Doncaster for scrapping. The shed at York now forms part of the NRM's annexe storage building.

Adding to the locomotive variety at York, Class 25/2 No. 25195 heads empty bogies on the goods avoiding line from Holgate Junction. The buildings in the background were once occupied by the former Railway Institute and Museum which closed its doors in 1973 for removal of exhibits in readiness for the NRM's opening two years later. It would appear that the NRM authorities have shown only a grudging interest in the declining diesel types, yet a home has been found for a Class 20, 31, 52 and 55 with the National Collection, together with their most recent addition – the veteran Class 40 pioneer No. 40122. It is expected that a Class 37 and a Class 47 will join them in the future, whilst the posterity of the gutsy 25s has been preserved elsewhere.

The change-over from semaphore signalling to multiple aspect colour lights at York was completed in 1951 when eight manual signal boxes were replaced by one electrically controlled box. It became the largest route relay interlocking scheme in the world covering 33 miles of track. At the time of writing, the 1950s equipment is being replaced in York's £18 million track and signalling modernisation scheme, covering an area from Northallerton in the north to Temple Hirst and Church Fenton in the south. Framed by the aged theatre type route indicators, 'Peak' class No. D128 (later 45145) heads a special to Scarborough on 30th May 1966. *Ian S. Carr*

From 1979 the entire Class 50 fleet passed through BREL Doncaster Works for heavy overhaul and repainting. The new livery was devised by BRB's Industrial Design Department following a request by BR's Chairman for a more imposing livery for main line diesels. The outshopped locomotives were returned to the WR by various routes, but usually diagrammed to work the 09.50 Edinburgh-Plymouth from York. On 3rd September 1981 it was the turn of No. 50045 *Achilles* seen here passing Holgate Junction.

## York – Selby

An unidentified Class 31 pulls out of the now-closed Dringhouses Yard in June 1984. During the '84 summer timetable the 'down' yard was used for recessing and wagon storage, whereas the 'up' yard had a hump and was bi-directional. Apart from exchanging traffic on twelve 'up' and thirteen 'down' trains, the yard also attached traffic originating from Rowntrees Mackintosh and the Carriage Works. The onset of electrification has now transformed the scene with catenary supports and overhead wires. By the 1970s, much of the ECML had already been rationalised with the exception of Newcastle and York, and a major re-modelling of trackwork was necessary to facilitate the new electric service.

A northbound IC125 accelerates from Chaloners Whin Junction in June 1983. Following the completion of the new 23 kilometre line to avoid the Selby Coalfield, BR engineers quickly re-claimed redundant ECML track south of Chaloners Whin Junction. No formal notice of withdrawal of service was required as the closure of the route was decreed in the private act of Parliament for construction of the diversion. The last day of operations was on 24th September 1983.

A general view of the specially designed turnouts at Colton North Junction at the northern end of the ECML Selby Coalfield diversion. The new line was built to enable the National Coal Board to mine a mile wide belt of coal, and to avoid the risk of mining subsidence seriously affecting the fast InterCity service on the original line, During the summer of 1983, BR introduced an intensive staff route training programme, using two withdrawn Craven Class 105 units and involving train crew men from BR's Doncaster, Leeds, King's Cross and Newcastle divisions. One of the twins, renumbered TDB 977124 and TDB 977125 in the departmental fleet approaches the newly-installed junction in August 1983. Colton North Junction is the longest and fastest on the BR network and is specifically designed for 125 mph running. The York-Leeds and Sheffield lines can be seen in the background.

*Left:* The 1963 Beeching mandate of re-shaping British Railways had been clear enough – to make the railways pay. Yet unlike our European counterparts it gave little concession for providing a public service. History has revealed the hypocrisy of it all, because Beeching wasted no time, and issued hundreds of closure notices throughout the Yorkshire region. Despite fierce public opposition, many Yorkshire stations were closed, but surprisingly some stations survived. Ulleskelf was one of them, and today its remote platform provides a valuable rail link for local inhabitants, particularly during the winter months when adverse weather can isolate the village for days on end. On such an occasion, a Class 47 heads towards York in freezing snow in 1981.

In the halcyon days of steam, the small village of Church Fenton enjoyed an impressive series of connections to York, Leeds, Sheffield and to Harrogate via the Wetherby branch. Today, the station retains many of its fine buildings, but the elaborate connections have long since disappeared. With the power handle opened up, Class 45 No. 45148 heads the 14.23 Newcastle-Paignton on 6th June 1982. Before the IC125s were introduced on the NE-SW service, the 'Peaks' made the cross-country route very much their own. They were in front line duty for over a decade, producing consistently good performances since the start of the 1961 summer timetable.

Displaced by IC125s on the ECML, the 'Deltics' could be found on varying duties during their final years. In this view, the operating department has provided ample power as 'Deltic' class No. 55008 *The Green Howards* heads two parcel vans at Church Fenton on 16th May 1981. The move was probably effected to re-position motive power with the 'Deltic' returning to its new depot at York. The lines to Leeds can be seen on the right.

*Opposite page top:*
Substantial quantities of steel are moved by block trains between the various production and finishing plants throughout the country. The steady procession of air-braked bogie wagons, especially converted for the movement of steel coils, earn BR's railfreight business considerable revenue. Waking up the residents of Church Fenton, a pair of Class 31s with No. 31282 leading, head the 6M47 Lackenby (Teesside)-Corby BSC steel coil train on the morning of 1st June 1981.

*Opposite page bottom:*
Class 45 No. 45121 heads the 09.50 Edinburgh-Plymouth through Monk Fryston in June 1981. The addition of a white stripe to the original lining band and cantrail was an unofficial livery variation which temporarily revived the otherwise dull overall blue of the 1965 corporate identity scheme. In the background, new sidings have been installed to replace those at Gascoigne Wood to facilitate traffic from the new Selby Coalfield. Now that the coalfield is fully operational, it is anticipated that BR will carry over 10 million tonnes of coal a year from the rapid coal terminal to Eggborough and Drax Power Stations.

# Selby Swing Bridge

*Above:*
Cautiously negotiating the swing bridge, 'Deltic' No. 55013 *The Black Watch* slows for the required stop at Selby on the 09.20 Newcastle-King's Cross. Opened in 1891, the bridge became well known by its ECML location. Consisting of five sections, including a main span 130ft long, a 92 ton weight is provided at the north end of the structure to balance its unequal central pivot 85ft by 45ft across the River Ouse.

*Left:*
The decision to re-route the ECML between York and Doncaster was conducive to both the National Coal Board and British Rail. It favoured BR's purpose by the introduction of faster timings over the new line. Before the diversionary route came into operation, IC125s had to slow to 40 mph for the swing bridge at Selby. With the station visible in the background, an unidentified Class 37 rattles across the structure in July 1982.

# West Yorkshire

Following local Government re-organisation of 1974, West Yorkshire became the largest of the six Metropolitan county's in land area, covering 787 square miles and with the third largest population of the six. The implementation of local Government brought with it a Passenger Transport Executive to integrate local road and rail passenger services within its area. However, the WYPTE had a particularly difficult task due to the geographical lie of the multi-centred conurbation, but their success in forming an efficient rail transport policy can be judged by the number of new stations which have been opened.

The first diesel multiple unit operation on British Railways was introduced in West Yorkshire on the service between Bradford Exchange-Leeds Central and Harrogate in April 1954. It was followed by an influx of dmu classes for branch line and local services throughout the region, but despite considerable savings in operating costs, many local passenger services and station closures were implemented.

InterCity connections are centred on Leeds with trains to Newcastle and the North, and to Sheffield-Birmingham and the West Country in the South. The north Pennine service still provides regular locomotive-hauled trains whilst the new 'Pacers' and 'Sprinters' are beginning to take-over almost all short and long distance services in the Provincial Sector. One of the most significant changes to train services in the region is the £306 million ECML electrification scheme which connects Leeds to the main line at Doncaster, and displaces Neville Hill's allocation of IC125s, which have dominated the Leeds-Bradford-King's Cross service since May 1979.

On the freight scene, there is an infinite variety of traffic to be found in the region, including a constant procession of

The contracting railway network can be seen in this view of Sowerby Bridge as a Class 37 with a brake tender, heads down the Calder Valley line with returning empties for Healey Mills. The decline of the Calder Valley line, dequadrified in 1965, culminated in 1970 with the withdrawal of York-Manchester trains via Normanton. On the left is the site of the former LYR locomotive depot which closed in January 1964.          *D. Green*

Following collision repairs at Stratford, the split headcode boxes at one end of Class 37 No. 37100 were replaced with built-in marker lights. The not-surprising resemblance to its departed Class 40 cousins can be seen at Castleford as it heads the 6L45 06.50 Derwenthaugh-Wakefield on 26th January 1983. *J. Wright*

mgr trains from the Yorkshire coalfield. With over 2,000 million tons at present known to be workable, the coalfield is the largest of any in Britain.

On the preservation front, the Middleton Railway Trust operates an industrial railway in south Leeds. It is claimed to be the world's oldest operating railway as an act of Parliament was authorised in 1758 to take coal in horse drawn trucks from the pits at Belle Isle and Middleton down to Leeds. Another preservation society operates the $4\frac{3}{4}$ mile long branch between Keighley and Oxenhope. Formed in 1962 it has become a popular tourist attraction in the heart of 'Bronteland'. The Keighley & Worth Valley Railway is essentially a steam operated line with a diesel railbus service at off-peak periods, but to placate the growing band of diesel preservationists, several shunters and a Class 25, No. 25059 have now been acquired for regular service on the line.

On the border of West and South Yorkshire, Class 56 No. 56094 heads mgr empties for Frickley Colliery on 23rd April 1983. Moorthorpe station platforms are visible in the background.

Literally the end of the line at Clayton West, now that passenger services have been withdrawn from the branch in January 1983. Here, a Class 110 dmu forming the 12.55 to Huddersfield stands in drizzly rain at the remote terminus in March 1982.
*P. Harris*

# Early Diesels-Leeds Area

A period view of the last years of steam showing the complex of lines radiating from Leeds City station. In 1967, the station was extensively rebuilt in the Leeds rationalisation scheme when trackwork was replanned to accommodate the newly-installed link from Whitehall Junction. Leeds Central station closed in May 1967 and all Leeds traffic was concentrated on City station. Here, steam is much in evidence as a departing Metro-Cammell 4-car set outpaces a Stanier tank towards Whitehall Junction, whilst a WD 2-8-0 heads a rake of coal wagons on the goods avoiding line towards Stourton in the distance. The scene has been completely transformed with steel masts and a curtain of overhead wires for the £306 million ECML electrification scheme connecting Leeds with the main line at Doncaster.

A major engineering feature of the Leeds-Harrogate line is Bramhope Tunnel which was built on a falling gradient northwards beneath the ridge separating the Aire and Wharfe valleys. Its construction was beset with problems when 23 men lost their lives, and a replica of the northern tunnel entrance stands as a monument in an Otley churchyard. Here, a green-liveried Class 108 2-car unit runs downhill on the 12.15 Leeds-Skipton which operated via Otley and Ilkley on the former NER and MR route through Wharfedale. The service became a casualty of the Beeching era when passenger services were withdrawn on 20th March 1965.

The differences in the front ends of the 'Peaks' can be seen in this view at Holbeck shed in July 1965. The initial batch of ten BR Derby Sulzer powered Type 4s were followed by 183 production loco-motives, uprated to 2,500hp and similar in appearance to the pilot scheme, except for front end variations when the gangway doors and white headcode discs were abandoned. Here, No. D152 (left) has its route indicator centrally placed, while the earlier production 'Peaks' Nos D26 and D29 appear with divided headcodes. The reporting numbers are: 1M86 southbound ''Thames Clyde Express'', 1S49 10.25 Leeds-Glasgow and 0L50 light engine Leeds Division. Note the shed allocation discs (55A) Holbeck on the warning panels. Leeds Holbeck was reduced in status to a re-fuelling post in 1975 and its remaining 20 'Peaks' were transferred to York.

*Left:*

Diverted because of engineering work on Sunday 7th April 1962, 'Deltic' class No. D9010 comes off the single-track Kippax branch at Garforth with the 10.10 King's Cross-Leeds. Introduced to traffic at Haymarket in July 1961, No. D9010 carries the pleasing two-tone green livery that adorned the new 'Deltics' and particularly suited their enormous bulk. The locomotive did not receive its *The King's Own Scottish Borderer* nameplates until May 1965 at a ceremony held at Dundee. Regimental names were bestowed on the Scottish and North Eastern Region 'Deltics' whilst the Eastern named their allocation after racehorses. (A view of a rather dejected looking No. 55010 can be seen on page 125 before it was broken up at Doncaster Works in May 1982). *J.M. Rayner*

*Left below:*

This early 1960's view of Holbeck shed evokes memories of the transition from steam as 'Peak' class No. D148 (later 46011) is seen passing Engine Shed Junction on the MR main line in July 1963. In the background, Stanier Black 5s stand in the shed yard with a pair of Class 25s and a solitary Class 03 shunter with its distinctive striped cab. The survival of the Black 5s during the last years of steam is testimony to the Stanier design, and comparisons to the performance of the general purpose mixed traffic Class 47 have emerged since dieselisation. Holbeck shed closed to steam on 30th September 1967, and three years later the roundhouse buildings and No. 1 type coaling tower were demolished.

*Below:*

Introduced in 1960, the Birmingham Railway Carriage & Wagon Co., TOPS Class 110 3-car sets were built specifically for the steeply-graded Calder Valley line across the Pennines. In January 1962, the Leeds-Bradford-Manchester route was served by an hourly service with some trains running throughout between Harrogate and Liverpool. With its roller blind slightly askew, DMC(L) vehicle No. 51841 leads a 6-car formation out of Bramhope Tunnel in June 1962.

The MR main line north of Leeds follows the easily-graded route along the Aire valley as far as Skipton. At the turn of the century the line was increased to four tracks from Leeds to Shipley involving the construction of a fly-over junction at Kirkstall to segregate local Bradford trains from through traffic to Scotland. With the "Waverley" express train headboard attached to the nose-end, 'Peak' class No. D30 heads northbound past the junction in July 1961. The express was withdrawn on closure of the Waverley route in 1969.

*Above:*
The yellow warning panel and off-white lining of the Brush Type 2 A1A-A1As can be clearly seen as No. D5858 climbs towards Thorner with a returning Wetherby-Heeley (Sheffield) race special on 3rd June 1963. This was probably the last race special over the Wetherby branch before the line closed to passenger traffic in January the following year. Despite the forward visibility afforded by the diesel cab, it would seem that old habits die hard for this train crew man is in typical footplate pose from steam days! *M. Mitchell*

*Right:*
Station closures are not exclusive to Beeching! The weed-ridden track on either side of the main line at Beeston Junction was once the start of the fly-over junction with the Batley branch which closed to passenger traffic in 1951. Here, a Calder Valley 3-car set heads towards Leeds in August 1963.

*Opposite page bottom:*
With the Leeds city landscape visible in the background, EE Co. Type 4 No. D246 (later 40046) climbs towards Morley with the 09.15 SO Leeds-Llandudno on 8th July 1967. Compared with the newer and more efficient design of later diesel classes, the cumbersome Class 40s were overweight and underpowered for their size. Yet the longevity of these sturdy machines was a remarkable achievement indeed. No. D246 was introduced to NE traffic in November 1959 and survived for almost 28 years! Condemned in February 1983, the redundant locomotive was towed to the Ministry of Defence at Moreton-on-Lugg for training exercises. It languished at the MOD depot for nearly three years before being moved via Crewe, Doncaster, Goole and Swindon Works prior to its final journey to Vic Berry's yard at Leicester where it was broken up in June 1987. *M. Mitchell*

# Leeds-Bradford -Ilkley dmus

In January 1959 all local trains between Leeds and Bradford to Ilkley and Skipton were dieselised. Here, a Derby Class 108 2-car unit forming the Bradford Forster Square-Leeds City service is seen leaving Calverley & Rodley station in June 1964. The service was withdrawn on 22nd March 1965 involving closure of seven intermediate stations between Leeds and Bradford. The line was dequadrified between Leeds and Shipley in 1967, retaining loops at Kirkstall for freight traffic.

With the MR line now reduced to two tracks, a Class 108 dmu forms an Ilkley-Leeds train running down the Aire Valley near Calverley in October 1982. Although the aged dmus were a decade or more past their best, they continued to put sterling service over the route. In 1975, BR introduced a refurbishing programme for dmus, including repainting, improved heating and ventilation, soundproofing and general improvements to the interior. The treatment may have been tangible proof of the worthiness of the old stock, yet it served to underline the need for more modern vehicles. It was not until 1984 that the pioneer lightweight second-generation Class 141 was introduced.

Passenger rail services have been subject to political interference of the worst kind. The Government Grant, known as the Public Services Obligation continues to be cut back, whilst the PTAs, whose responsibility it is for financing local rail services in their area, urgently seek ways to operate efficient Metro train services, despite rising operating costs. The Ilkley line has seen better days. In the sylvan surroundings of the Wharfe Valley, an Ilkley-Leeds dmu is strengthened to a pair of twin units near Burley in Wharfedale in July 1963.

Exquisite detail of wrought iron, glass roofed canopy and gas lighting was to be found at the 'listed' Victorian station at Ilkley in October 1982. Here, a Metro-Cammell Class 101 dmu stands at the now-disused platform 3, once serving the through Midland line to Skipton which closed to passenger traffic in March 1965. At the time of writing, the station is undergoing restoration in conjunction with a shopping development, thus ending one of the last examples of platform gas-lighting in the country.

Main line steam died a lingering and painful death until their final departure in 1968. When the new diesels came to the fore, steam was quickly relegated to less demanding duties as the 'Peak' Type 4s began to dominate Anglo-Scottish expresses on the MR main line out of Leeds. They appeared with monotonous regularity from the beginning of 1961, displacing the BR 'Britannia' Standard Pacifics, together with the eight A3s transferred from Tyneside when the ECML was dieselised. Prior to the commencement of the 1961 summer timetable, BR/Sulzer Type 4s Nos D11 and D14 were allocated to Neville Hill shed for crew training purposes on the lines north of Leeds. 'Peak' class No. D14 is seen heading an interesting collection of articulated coaching stock at Apperley Bridge on the return working to Leeds.

Bradford Exchange station had ten platforms covered by a double arched roof measuring 450ft long and 100ft in span. By the 1960s, the condition of the roof was causing serious concern, and in 1973 an Infrastructure grant was announced towards a new Interchange station which was fully opened four years later. With the now demolished roof visible in the background, a brand new Brush Type 4 heads ecs out of Exchange in July 1966. Crewe-built No. D1999 was one of a batch of locomotives, Nos D1977-D1999 within the fleet allocated to 52A, Gateshead and 55B, York to work ECML services between Leeds-Newcastle and King's Cross. The initial batch allocations of the Class 47 was quickly eradicated when they emerged as the standard locomotive within the Type 4 category. They were then dispersed to every part of the network, not only to replace steam, but to substitute existing diesels.

*H. Malham*

Delivered to ER capital stock on 4th September 1961 English Electric 'Deltic' No. D9012 *Crepello* looks in pristine condition and devoid of any warning panel as it heads the Bradford portion of the 10.10 Leeds-King's Cross at Exchange station in October 1961. During the ensuing years the 3,300hp 'Deltics' were to become the thoroughbreds of the ECML when they ousted the Gresley Pacifics and EE Co. Type 4 D200s from front line duty. *H. Malham*

The long-expected announcement of BR's intention to withdraw Settle & Carlisle passenger traffic coincided with the introduction of the re-conditioned Class 40 No. 40122 (D200) into regular service on the line. The locomotive, based at Carlisle, worked the 10.40 Carlisle-Leeds and 16.00 return service. There is no concession for sentimentality they say, but the appearance of No. D200 on the line revived an otherwise gloomy year for S&C fans. The Class 40 looks resplendent in original green livery as it departs from the newly-erected platform at Shipley on the return trip to Carlisle in August 1983. The single-line platform was built in 1979 to avoid the untidy operation of reversal for the Leeds-Skipton dmu service.

*Opposite page top:*

An early liveried Class 108 2-car set with front end chevron and white roof, heads through Saltaire towards Shipley on the Skipton-Leeds service in June 1961. In the background can be seen part of Sir Titus Salt's mill complex, regarded as one of the finest examples of an intact Victorian Industrial Village and designated a conservation area by the Department of Environment. Saltaire station was demolished soon after the withdrawal of local passenger trains in 1965. The service was resumed in 1984 when the WYPTE financed a new station, built generously in local stone to comply with the conservation standards laid down for the ten acre 'Palace of Industry'.

*Opposite page bottom:*

The details of this picture make interesting reading as the now dequadrified line between Bingley and Keighley is occupied by the new Crossflats station which was opened by the WYPTE in 1982. On 17th March 1965, a rather grimy Class 25, No. D7587 is seen en route from Derby to Hellifield with two immaculate MR locomotives and LTSR *Thundersley,* in tow. The antiques were to be stored at Hellifield steam shed alongside other preserved steam locomotives before their dispersal to more permanent homes. Although Hellifield shed had been closed for two years, the depot building was still intact with a complete roof and glazed windows, but as a further precaution BR secured windows and doors with 3 x 2 batons and six inch nails to keep out intruders!

*H. Malham*

## KWVR

The British Railways modernisation programme of 1959 included plans for a lightweight railbus service on selected Eastern Region branch lines. The vehicles chosen for the experiment were the four-wheeled design built by WMD at Donauwurth in West Germany and used on German Federal Railways. The five railbuses (Nos E79960-E79964) were withdrawn in 1967 and a pair found their way to the KWVR for use on the year-round off-peak service between Keighley and Oxenhope. The control gear of the two railbuses has been modified so that they can be coupled together and used as a multiple unit. In this view, Nos DRB62 (E79962) and DRB64 (E79964) are confronted in the shed yard at Haworth by another foreign import in the shape of the ex USA 2-8-0 "Big Jim" No. 5820.

*P. Harris*

Although Keighley station has retained many of its fine buildings, the difference in the decor of the BR station and the adjoining KWVR terminus is immediately apparent to visitors descending from street level to the platform. It has taken many years of renovation by the KWVR staff to restore the ex MR canopy and station buildings to their former state, whereas the BR station looks very plain in comparison. With the KWVR/BR rail connection visible in the background, a 3-car Metro-Cammell unit forms the service to Bradford Forster Square.

*Below and right:*
In the days before rationalisation came into common parlance, the station at Halifax could boast Dining and Refreshment Rooms, Waiting Rooms, Ladies Rooms, Bookstalls and platforms giving connections to every part of the region. The once grandiose station has now fallen into a state of decay and Calderdale Council has launched an Inheritance Project in an effort to enhance the town's image. It includes the restoration of the 1855 station building and re-instatement of main platforms. *Below:* A then brand new Metro-Cammell Class 101 in dark Brunswick green livery, awaits departure from platform 3 at Halifax in July 1959. *Right:* The decline of Halifax's rail traffic can be seen in this splendid aerial view showing the rationalisation of trackwork once radiating from the station. The coal staithes and sidings are empty, and the Class 03 shunter at the top, left of the picture has only minor duties to perform in the goods yard which eventually closed in December 1980.
*Both: D. Green*

# Pennine Routes

The first Trans-Pennine railway to enter West Yorkshire was the Manchester-Leeds Railway in 1841. The line was built by George Stephenson and passes through the upper reaches of the Calder Valley by way of Todmorden and Sowerby Bridge. Here, the 13.58 Manchester-Leeds drops down to Todmorden from the 2,885 yard long Summit Tunnel. In December 1984 the tunnel was the scene of a major accident when a train of oil tankers derailed and the petroleum product ignited causing an inferno lasting several days. Smoke and flames belched from the ventilation shafts and the intense heat caused part of the brick lining to vitrify. When the fire had died down an inspection of the tunnel revealed that damage was less than expected, and seven months later the service between Manchester and Leeds was resumed.

In the foreground is Gauxholme Viaduct which carries the railway over the Rochdale Canal. The original turreted skew bridge consisted of a self-contained iron arched bridge that supported the deck system by means of hangers, but was re-inforced with girders by the LMS in 1905.

Still in green livery, EE Co. Type 3 Co-Co No. D6938 is assisted at the rear by Class 8F 2-8-0 No. 48167 on the climb to Copy Pit summit with a coal train from the West Riding on 19th July 1968. The L&Y line over Copy Pit was once a major rail artery which linked the Lancashire towns of Burnley, Blackburn and Preston with the Yorkshire towns along the Calder Valley. The route fell into gradual decline with the withdrawal of local passenger services and it became a mere freight-only link in the backwater of the BR system. At the beginning of the winter 1984 timetable the line was revived with the introduction of the 'Roses Rail Link' dmu service between Leeds, Bradford and Preston.
*M. Mitchell*

In 1962, an hourly dmu service was introduced between Leeds, Bradford and Manchester via the Calder Valley line. The service was dominated by the 3-car 720hp units built by the Birmingham Railway Carriage & Wagon Company. Here, a Leeds-Manchester Class 110 heads towards Sowerby Bridge in July 1984. The regularity of the units over the route coined their name the 'Calder Valley' sets, now displaced by Class 150/1 'Sprinters' which began operations across the Pennines in 1987. The Calder Valley line has now been revived as a premier freight route enabling the introduction of accelerated passenger services on the re-vamped main Trans-Pennine route via Huddersfield.

In recent years the LNWR line has emerged as the principal east-west route across the Pennines. The line enters West Yorkshire through the watershed at Standedge before sweeping down the Calder Valley to Huddersfield. Construction of the line involved considerable building work, including two single bore tunnels and a double tunnel when the line was quadrupled throughout. Here, a Class 47 sweeps into West Yorkshire with a loose coupled freight in June 1983.

*Opposite page top:*
The traditional image of West Yorkshire as a continuous sprawl of mill chimneys and terraced houses is best found in the Colne and Calder valleys. The influence of the builders is so profound, that even today, despite their filth and neglect, many once proud Victorian buildings stand as a monument to their work. In this view, the 'old' Sowerby Bridge architecture has given way to newly-erected factories which occupy the site of the L&Y steam shed closed in 1964. A Manchester-Halifax-Bradford-Leeds dmu heads down the Calder Valley in July 1983.

Westbound traffic is faced with a ruling gradient of 1 in 105 from Huddersfield and goods trains are able to seek refuge on the loop from Marsden which rejoins the main line at Standedge Tunnel. Framed by the overbridge carrying overspill water from a nearby reservoir, Class 45 No. 45111 *Grenadier Guardsman* emerges from Stanhedge Tunnel with the 12.05 Liverpool-Scarborough in May 1983. On the right is the disused Huddersfield Narrow Canal, less than 7ft wide, which enters the hillside through a 5,456 yard long bore at a lower level beneath the railway.

The 1979 timetable saw the appearance of Class 47 haulage and Mk2 coaching stock on a much-improved hourly service between York and Manchester via Standedge. Cautiously negotiating Marsden's reverse curves, No. 47510 *Fair Rosamund* runs downhill with the 15.05 Bangor-Scarborough in August 1983. The route was reduced to two tracks in 1966 enabling BR engineers to slew existing lines across the quadrupled trackbed to ease speed restrictions. From May 1987, the Standedge route has undergone a major facelift with the introduction of dmu Class 150/2 'Sprinters' between York, Leeds, Manchester and Liverpool, whilst Newcastle trains continue to be operated by a dedicated fleet of Class 47s based at Gateshead.

Modellers seeking a solution to the prototypical appearance of fiddle yard entrances should study this view, taken from above Huddersfield and Gledholt tunnels where the Penistone line diverges from Springhead Junction and crosses the Calder Valley by Paddock Viaduct. The 13 mile route is heavily engineered with six tunnels and four viaducts. In the foreground, an unidentified Class 37 heads mgr empties for Healey Mills out of Gledholt Tunnel towards Huddersfield.

The lines from Huddersfield join the Calder Valley lines at a much-changed Heaton Lodge Junction. In 1965, BR engineers re-modelled the junction by incorporating the underpass once used by the LNWR for their Spen Valley route to Leeds. The 1960's junction enabled InterCity trains on the Stanhedge route to avoid Calder Valley traffic by fly-under. Class 37 No. 37061 heads the 13.59 SO Blackpool-Sheffield down the Calder Valley towards Mirfield on 6th July 1985. The junction was further rationalised in 1987 when the fly-under junction was singled for eastbound traffic only.

Huddersfield station can boast a façade over 400ft long with a central portico 68ft high; all of it supported by eight stately columns. The magnificent frontage is somewhat compromised by the interior of the station which has been reduced in the number of used platforms and part of the train shed roof has been removed. Here, the exposed girders cast light and shade on Class 47 No. 47482 arriving with the 13.32 Newcastle-Liverpool on 8th May 1983.

# Pennine Peaks

Displaced by IC125s on the Midland route, the redundant Class 45/1s were drafted on to the Trans-Pennine service from 1981. A year later, East-West trains formerly terminating at York were extended to Scarborough to improve stock utilisation. From May 1987, the aged Class 45/1s were being phased out with the introduction of middle distance 'Sprinters' on an intensive half-hourly service between Leeds and Manchester. *Above:* Passing the site of the ex-LYR steam shed at Mirfield, No. 45115 heads the 09.35 SO Newcastle-Liverpool on the now-dequadrified line to Heaton Lodge Junction on 15th February 1985. The rationalisation was coincident with re-modelling Thornhill Junction, raising the speed limit from 45mph to 65mph to facilitate the new Trans-Pennine timetable. *Left:* No. 45019 heads the 10.05 Liverpool-Scarborough towards Dewsbury in March 1985. The single line in the foreground once formed the L&Y route to Low Moor which closed to traffic in 1961. It now provides a rail link to Hargreaves Oil Terminal at Liversedge and is used 'as required' by a nominal amount of traffic.

# Trans-Pennine 1960s

At the beginning of 1961, an hourly service of 3-car dmus commenced between Leeds and Huddersfield. It was complemented by a two-hourly service throughout to Manchester. In this view, a 3-car Metro-Cammell set making up the 09.50 Leeds City-Manchester Exchange restarts from Ravensthorpe station in April 1962. On the right are the Calder Valley lines, now reduced to three tracks, looking towards Healey Mills and the site of the ex-LYR Thornhill station which closed in 1952. The aged semaphores were replaced when signalling came under the control of the power box at Healey Mills in 1970.

January 1961 saw the start of Class 40 haulage on the Newcastle-Liverpool service over the Standedge route. Type 4 1Co-Co1 No. D277 heads the 11.00 Liverpool-Newcastle near Lady Anne Crossing between Dewsbury and Leeds on 6th August 1966. In the background can be seen the lattice girder which carried the GNR Bradford-Dewsbury-Wakefield line down into Batley. The line was closed to passengers in December 1965.

*M. Mitchell*

Construction of Healey Mills Marshalling Yard began in 1959, involving the diversion of the River Calder and the re-routing of the 'up' and 'down' lines which enclosed a total of 140 acres of sidings. The yard was opened in 1963 by Lord Robens, then Chairman of the National Coal Board. The 1980's re-organisation of Speedlink has seen a complete decline in wagonload traffic operations and consequently many marshalling yard facilities have now been withdrawn. In 1984, the hump at Healey Mills was closed and the diesel depot was reduced in status from a Traction Maintenance Depot to a Servicing Depot. Very much on home ground, Class 56 No. 56118 eases mgr empties on to the 'down' line in May 1983. HM depot is reached by the footbridge in the background.

## Wakefield Area

*Opposite page top:*
At near zero temperatures, the winter sunrise reveals a line-up of redundant diesel locomotives awaiting a decision on their future in December 1983. They included the Class 24 No. ADB 968009 (D5142), broken up at Coopers Yard in September 1984, whereas the Class 15 No. ADB 968001 (D8233) was to find a new lease of life under the auspices of the South Yorkshire Preservation Society's HQ at Chapletown, Sheffield, but later moved to Bury. Amongst the line-up are several doomed Class 40s, once HM's proud workhorse when the depot housed a sizeable stud to handle the heavy freight traffic from the yard.

*Opposite page bottom:*
Veteran Class 40 No. 40003 heads a motley collection of wagons through Horbury Cutting towards Healey Mills on 15th May 1981. This locomotive, alias No. D203, was one of the ten EE Co. Type 4 pilot scheme locomotives, introduced in 1958 and allocated to Stratford and Hornsey depots on the ER. The aged locomotive has retained the gangway doors and folding headcode discs as built, but by the time this photograph was taken its life expiry was due when BR's policy of withdrawal of the class based on works dates was advocated. Due to power shortages some Class 40s survived out of sequence and No. 40003 was not withdrawn until August 1982.

Following an earthslip on the MR line at Royston in October 1982, the North East – South West service between Sheffield and York was diverted via Pontefract, whilst the service to Leeds was re-routed via Moorthorpe and Wakefield. Two years later, the InterCity sector made significant changes to the service north of Sheffield by retaining the Leeds diversion, but re-routing York trains through Doncaster. Not only did it enable BR to save further expenditure on track and signalling to upgrade the MR route for the benefit of HSTs but it also provided an opportunity of focussing ECML and Humberside connections on the North East – South West service at Doncaster. In this view, a northbound IC125 is diverted back to its original route due to engineering work at Moorthorpe on 6th June 1983, and is seen passing Royston Junction cabin on the former MR line, just north of Cudworth.

At the turn of the century, several railway companies increased trackwork over existing routes to assist the flow of traffic from other regions. The LYR quadrupled most of the route between Brighouse and Horbury, whilst the LMS later completed the widening to Wakefield. It involved opening out of the 128yd tunnel at Horbury to a four tracked cutting. The four tracks were paired by direction with the fast lines in the centre. A Class 47 heads empty mgr hoppers from Healey Mills in March 1982.

*Opposite page:* The once-busy Healey Mills Marshalling Yard provided an infinite variety of freight traffic, this one being comprised of newly-repaired HAA hoppers from Knottingley. Contrary to appearance, the Class 08 shunter is propelling its train towards Horbury Station Junction in the background. The line diverging on the left is the freight-only spur to Crigglestone and Barnsley in South Yorkshire, whilst in the background is the site of Horbury and Ossett station which closed in 1970. The station had an island platform served by the fast lines only.

A Sheffield-Barnsley-Leeds dmu approaches Horbury Junction on 18th March 1985. The tracks curving away to the right head towards Healey Mills with the Procor Wagon Works at the apex of the junction. Horbury Junction was once the site of the LYR station, closed in 1927 and replaced by Horbury Mirfield Road Station nearer to the town. On the horizon, left can be seen the 1,080ft Emley Moor Transmitter which came into operation in 1971. It replaced an earlier Independent Television Authority mast which collapsed three years earlier.

By the mid-1980s the ranks of operational Class 40s had diminished to only a handful making it to 1985. Eking out its final days, No. 40192 heads through Wakefield Kirkgate on 7th January 1985. The locomotive was one of the final batch of Class 40s, Nos 40145-40199 fitted with a single four-character headcode display panel. When headcode displays were abolished in 1976, they were replaced by a black panel with two translucent holes which were illuminated by the original panel lights. In the background is the GNR viaduct on the Wakefield Westgate-Doncaster line, now adorned with catenary masts for the ECML electrification to Leeds.

*Opposite page:*
Passing the once-numerous semaphores at Goosehill Junction, a Sheffield-Leeds dmu heads towards Normanton on 20th April 1982. The dmu has just crossed from the right hand pair of tracks from Wakefield Kirkgate. The lines on the left once formed the MR main line to Sheffield via Cudworth, but these were lifted in March 1988 during a major remodelling of trackwork. This included the removal of semaphore signalling and the introduction of colour light MAS.

In 1974 West Yorkshire was split into five Metropolitan districts; Calderdale, Kirklees, Bradford, Leeds and Wakefield. Its inherent rail routes posed many problems for the newly-formed PTE and it was feared that the needs of local bus passenger services would take precedence over those of local rail services in the region. However, the opening of new stations and the subsequent increase in local rail passengers has completely vindicated the PTE's involvement in BR's operation. Class 37 No. 37215 holds up the bus service at Streethouse level crossing as it heads towards Wakefield on 15th November 1982. The pit spoil heap in the background is a common sight in the coalfield, but a programme of reclamation has greatly reduced the number in recent years.

*J. Wright*

Comparisons are odious, they say, but there are occasions when the truth must be told, and the terrible state of neglect of BR property is a case in point. You do not have to go too far out of your way to find unfavourable comparisons with the so-called 'modern image.' Normanton for example. Once an important railway centre, enjoying early importance as a refreshment stop on MR Anglo-Scottish expresses, it now stands in a dilapidated condition as a Class 37 heads towards Goose Hill Junction with a ballast train in April 1982.

Diverted because of engineering work at Leeds Neville Hill, 'Peak' class No. 45104 *Royal Warwickshire Fusiliers* heads the 08.40 Liverpool-York past Castleford on 12th June 1983. BR engineers occupied the line until noon, and all east-west InterCity services were reversed at Leeds, then diverted via Methley Junction to regain the York lines at Church Fenton. The re-routing was coincident with the annual air display at Church Fenton, causing further delays when InterCity traffic was scheduled to stop for visitors to the show. Some trains were running up to an hour late at York.

# Knottingley– Moorthorpe

*Opposite page, top:* The diesel depot at Knottingley, is situated at the heart of the complex of lines from the South Yorkshire Coalfield to the Airedale power stations of Eggborough, Drax and Ferrybridge. With the cooling towers of Ferrybridge on the horizon, a line-up of Class 56s rest between duties, including Crewe-built No. 56129 – identified by the silver painted grille on the bodyside, and No. 56074 *Kellingley Colliery*, (beyond No. 56003 on the right) one of a pair of 56s fitted with a remote control system and yellow roof mounted beacons.

*Opposite page, bottom:*
Standing 300ft high and each weighing almost 5,000 tonnes, the cooling towers of Ferrybridge Power Station provide an unusual backdrop as Class 31 No. 31162 heads a train of mixed ballast hoppers towards York on 25th May 1981. The Ferrybridge complex consists of three stations: A, B and C. The latter was opened in 1966 with the capacity of producing 2,000 megawatts. In all, the Aire Valley stations can produce 12,500 megawatts, much of it exported via the grid system to other parts of Britain, and all of it requiring a constant procession of mgr trains to feed their insatiable appetite for coal.

The old cliché 'Familiarity breeds contempt' should apply to the Class 47s because their considerable numbers, total built 512, gave rise to their nickname 'Duffs' by some enthusiasts. Yet, the traditional hardiness of the Brush design was established early on when they were adopted as the standard Type 4. At the southern extreme of the West Yorkshire network, a Class 47 heads the 17.30 Leeds-Bristol on the spur from the GNR Leeds-Doncaster route to the York-Sheffield lines at Moorthorpe. Since the diversion of the NE-SW expresses via Doncaster the operating costs of the York-Sheffield line falls mainly on local passenger trains which is unsupported by any of the local transport authorities through which the service runs.

On 24th May 1983, Class 46 No. 46018 heads the diverted 11.05 Penzance-Leeds through Moorthorpe. During their final years, the Class 46s were in a poor state and by the time this photograph was taken the fleet was almost entirely replaced by IC125s on the MR line. Main generator problems further depleted the ranks, and this particular locomotive, introduced in February 1962 as No. D155, was finally withdrawn from service in December 1984.

# North Humberside

The following pages are devoted to an area of North Humberside which was formed as part of the 1974 Local Government re-organisation, covering a region lying on both sides of the Humber estuary.

Kingston upon Hull, to give it its proper name, is the main city of Humberside, situated on the outer bend of the estuary, which provides a deep water channel for shipping. At the turn of the century, the port was developed into one of the most important railway/shipping centres in the north east of England when the NER and Hull & Barnsley Railway built a series of dock lines to facilitate the increased rail traffic from the hinterland.

Dieselisation came to the region when a new dmu service began operations in the Hull area in January 1957. Despite the reduced costs and economies of pay-train operations, the new dmus were unable to eradicate the losses of some lines, and in October 1964, the Withernsea and Hornsey branches were closed, followed a year later by the withdrawal of passenger services via Market Weighton in the heart of the Yorkshire Wolds.

For over a decade, much of the rail traffic originating from Hull docks has been taken over by road haulage involving the removal of hundreds of miles of redundant sidings, together with the closure of mpds at Alexander Dock, Springhead, Dairycoates, and more recently Botanic Gardens – once famed for its Trans-Pennine dmu allocation.

Today, the railway network of Hull has reached austere levels which clearly reflects the economic state of BR's operation. At the same time, it betrays the Government's stubborn refusal to recognise the advantage of moving heavy goods by rail. Indeed one has only to compare the motorway extravagances in the region to illustrate the point!

The navigational channel of the Humber estuary is constantly changing its course and daily surveys are necessary to measure the shift of mud washed up by the tides from Holderness. High tides occur twice a day, deepening the channel which enables large ships to navigate the River Ouse as far as Selby. Modern ships have to be fast enough to make the passage during high water, steering a course through the swing bridge which carries the Hull-Doncaster line across the Ouse near Goole. The moving span of the bridge has girders 251ft long by 16ft deep and weighs 650 tons. It turns on 36 rollers which provide two 100ft openings for shipping. In recent years, the bridge has seen more than its share of mishaps from collision by ships, and during the early 1980s the estimated cost of repairing the weakened structure raised serious doubts about the future of the line. In this view, the damaged wooden jetty can be clearly seen as a Hull-Doncaster dmu heads across the swing span towards Goole in July 1983.

When BR revealed the poor condition of the Ouse swing bridge and their intention to close the line, it aroused heated protests from the North Humberside community. An action group was formed – known irreverently as 'Goolies' – who raised more than 3,000 objections to the closure. Humberside County Council eventually reached financial agreement with BR, and in 1985 the closure plan was dropped. Had it gone ahead, Hull trains would have been diverted via Selby, whilst the service from Doncaster would have terminated at Goole. Here, a Class 37 heads the 6M87 Hull-Spondon tanks through Goole in May 1983.

The flat landscape of Hull necessitates numerous level crossings in the area. Road traffic is delayed at Walton Street crossing as 'Peak' class No.45140 heads the 14.40 SO Scarborough-Luton towards Hull on 3rd September 1983. This summer-only service avoided Hull's Paragon station by taking the spur at Anlaby Road Junction to gain lines out of the city.

Goole is the most inland port on the east coast of Britain and to reach it, ships have to sail 50 miles along the Humber river from the North Sea. There are 37 acres of docks which handle over 2,000 vessels and more than 1.5 million tonnes a year. *Above:* Lofty cranes dominate the Goole landscape as Class 08s rest between duties at Goole Goods Junction on 29th October 1983. *Below:* In the opposite direction, Class 37s Nos 37008 and 37106 stand at Goole's stabling point on the same day. The empty sidings bear silent witness to the decline of rail traffic to the port.

# Goole-Gilberdyke

Following the opening of the direct route from Doncaster via Goole, the line to Hull was widened from Gilberdyke Junction through sparsely populated countryside to Hessle East. In recent years, much of the line has been de-quadrified, yet it has always remained the most important route into the city. *Above:* Flanked by semaphores, a 5-car Hull-Leeds dmu heads across the flat Humberside landscape towards Gilberdyke on 1st August 1983. *Below:* In the opposite direction, migrating birds are startled to flight as a Metro-Cammell 2-car set rattles non-stop past Gilberdyke on the Leeds-Hull service. The lines to Goole diverge left beyond the road overbridge.

The north Humberside landscape is flat and featureless, and seldom an attraction for photographers, yet there is an interesting variety of locations to be found in the region. Regaining speed after the Brough stop, Class 31 No.31448 hurries past Ferriby with the 15.41 Manchester-Hull on 2nd June 1984. It was the first year of the re-instatement of locomotive-hauled trains over the Pennine routes, displacing the aged Trans-Pennine sets which had plied the arduous cross-country service for a quarter of a century. The even older Class 31s had been newly-equipped with eth but by the late 1980s, the introduction of the 'Sprinter' dmu fleet had rendered the Class 31/4s an expensive means of hauling provincial services stock, and as a result the locomotives have become surplus to requirements in recent years.

*Opposite page top:*
The Swindon-built 6-car Trans-Pennine sets were introduced in 1960, providing six trains each way daily betwen Hull and Liverpool via the Stanhedge route. They were allocated to Neville Hill brand new, but spent the remainder of their working lives at Hull Botanic Gardens depot. Here, as it will have done countless times before, a Class 124 set departs from Hull on 27th August 1983. The units were withdrawn from service in May 1984, but sadly none has been preserved.

*Opposite page bottom:*
Hull Paragon station was established on a 2¹/2 acre site in 1848, later extended by the NER at the turn of the century to cater for increased traffic radiating out of Hull. The magnificent overall roof consists of five lattice girder arches covering the platforms and two smaller roofs spanning the concourse. By 1977, the train shed was in poor condition and BR was granted Listed Building consent to embark on refurbishment of the deteriorating structure. Here, renovation is well under way as 'Deltic' class No. 55013 *The Black Watch* arrives on the 12.05 ex-King's Cross on 30th August 1980. *P. Harris*

*Top:* In October 1984, trackwork at the entrance to Paragon station was considerably simplified, replacing several double slips by one scissors crossover. The new trackwork controls all platforms and enables Selby-Doncaster trains to proceed independently from the Wolds Coast dmus to Bridlington and Scarborough. On 27th October rationalisation is well under way as Class 31/4 No. 31424 heads past Hull Paragon signal cabin with the 12.05 Hull-Manchester.

*Above:*
When British Railways adopted the name British Rail in 1965, they introduced the new twin arrow design as their symbol. In the same year, passenger services were withdrawn from many Yorkshire lines, including the Selby-Bridlington and York-Hull routes across the Yorkshire Wolds. The closures seriously exposed the Hull-Scarborough line to the same fate, but it was reprieved when the Minister of Transport refused to consent withdrawal. Here, a Scarborough-Hull dmu departs from Beverley across Grovehill Road in October 1984. The covered footbridge and overall roof at Beverley can be seen in the backround.

*Opposite page:*
The original North Eastern Railway station at Bridlington consisted of an overall roof covering two platforms, later extended by an additional six platforms for the NER excursion traffic to the resort. The roof was removed in 1961, followed by the now-all-too-familiar 1980s rationalisation to be found throughout the country's rail network. Here, 'Peak' class No.45140 approaches the station with the 14.40 SO Scarborough-Luton in September 1983. The lines curving to the right lead to the goods yard which was used to accommodate dmus staying-over during the summer months.

## Wolds Coast Line

# South Yorkshire

South Yorkshire was evolved out of part of the old West Riding which was bitterly and controversially abandoned in 1974. The new County comprises an area stretching from the Peak District National Park in the west, across the industrial landscape of Sheffield, Rotherham and Barnsley to the low level 'carrs' around Doncaster in the east.

Since the turn of the century, railway companies were quick to recognise the potential of the South Yorks wealth of coal deposits which compelled them to build a series of connecting lines penetrating every corner of the region. Many towns were served by duplicated routes as pre-Grouping companies competed for traffic originating from the coal mines and iron and steel foundries in the Don valley. In the meantime, Doncaster was developing rapidly as a major rail centre when the GNR established the famous 'plant' locomotive works.

The first regular dmu service was introduced between Sheffield and York in 1959. It was the beginning of a period when the railways in South Yorkshire saw significant changes with a heavy influx of diesels during the early 1960s, together with the development of the region's freight traffic at a new marshalling yard at Tinsley. At the same time, BR announced their intention to close the former Great Central main line with the withdrawal of the Sheffield Victoria-Manchester Piccadilly electric service via Woodhead.

During recent years, the decline of the steel industry and the exhaustion of coal reserves at some pits has seen the coincident fall in rail traffic. Sadly, the rail network of South Yorkshire has now reached a stage where the function it has performed since the turn of the century is of no further use, and BR has been forced to abandon such extravagances. Scenes of decrepid pit head gear, disused sidings and hundreds of acres of abandoned lines clearly reveal the industrial dross to be found in the region.

From the beginning of the 1980s, there have emerged some significant improvements of South Yorkshire's railways with the introduction of HSTs on the NE-SW service and the much-neglected Sheffield-London line, whilst local services are benefiting from new rolling stock. By far the biggest project is the ECML electrification which will herald a new generation of 140mph Class 91 Bo-Bo 'Electra' class locomotives and Mk 4 coaching stock to the region.

The southern approach to Tinsley Yard is severely graded, passing through a deep cutting, at one time containing a 26 siding secondary yard. The summit of the cutting fans out at the entrance to the main yard, approached here by a Class 37 heading a train of mixed ballast hoppers on 26th April 1983.

*Above:* A Class 31 heads a mixed freight on the GC route towards Rotherham in April 1983. In the background are the giant cooling towers of Tinsley Power Station and the double-deck viaduct of the M1 motorway.

*Above right:* The finished product is brand new, and yet to turn a wheel in revenue earning service; Class 58 No.58002 is reflected in the wall mirror at BREL's Doncaster Works on 13th May 1983.

*Below:* With revised centre indicator panel fitted with marker lights, Class 45 No.45031 heads past Wath Junction with T32 mgr empties to Manners Colliery on 13th April 1981.                                        *J. Wright*

# Barnsley Area

*Opposite page top:*
The proposal for closure of the Huddersfield-Sheffield via Penistone service has been a long and drawn out saga involving the PTAs of both South and West Yorkshire. As the Government Grant system does not apply to lines administered by a Passenger Transport Authority, then it is up to the PTAs to provide a subsidy to maintain local Metrotrains. BR were concerned that the WPTA's offer of financial support was insufficient to cover the Huddersfield-Denby Dale section, whereas the PTA argued that BR should give more support because the line was an integral part of the InterCity feeder network at Huddersfield. Cash support was withdrawn and the line went through the official closure procedure. In 1987, it was reprieved when BR agreed to put a ceiling on the annual PTA's subsidy, made possible by the introduction of lower running costs due to singling the line. With Peninstone Viaduct visible in the background, a departing Metro-Cammell dmu heads past the derelict North Box on the 13.42 to Huddersfield on 25th August 1969. The L&Y origin of the route is revealed by the Company's warning notice on the right. *Ian S. Carr*

*Opposite page bottom and below:*
During the 1980s, the former MR main line was still rich in semaphores and old style signal boxes. The area around Cudworth is covered by hundreds of acres of abandoned sidings which reveal the extent of railway operations at the turn of the century when Cudworth became the centre of Hull & Barnsley Railway activities. Following the withdrawal of local passenger services in January 1968, together with the 1980's diversion of main line trains to other routes, the railway centre at Cudworth is now a part of history. *Below left:* In the days before the diversions were introduced, Class 47 No.47567 heads past Cudworth North Junction on 21st April 1982. *Below:* A Class 45 negotiates South Junction with mgr empties on the same day.

The new Passenger Transport Authority, set up after the abolition of Metropolitan counties, is fortunate that most local Metrotrain services in South Yorkshire share tracks with InterCity trains. However, the SYPTA subsidises the seven mile section between Barnsley and Penistone which was brought into use from May 1983 for a new Sheffield-Huddersfield via Penistone service to include Barnsley. Soon after the service commenced, a Sheffield-bound Class 101 2-car set approaches Barnsley on 21st May 1983.

The Class 20s are normally used in multiple to provide sufficient power and brakeforce for heavy freight workings, but ample power is provided here for a train of redundant track at Mitchells Main Box near Wath. The leading locomotive, No.20132, is one of the final batch fitted with revised nose and cab ends to accommodate the four character identification panel, now displaced by two marker lights.

## Under the Wires

At the turn of the century, the Great Central Railway built a large marshalling yard at Wath in the centre of the South Yorkshire Coalfield to meet the increased demand for the movement of coal. Much of the yard's traffic was despatched westward over the Woodhead route, including the tortuous 1 in 40 Worsbrough Incline to Penistone. In 1952, the route was electrified between Wath and Dunford Bridge, and two years later the 1,500 volt dc system was completed throughout between Sheffield and Manchester. Here, a Class 37 heads a coal train from Elsecar Main Colliery to Wath Yard beneath the wires at Elsecar Junction.

*P. Harris*

A general view of the traction depot at Wath which stood on the perimeter of the marshalling yard, but provided only the minimum of accommodation in a two road corrugated asbestos shed. Diesel traction is considerably outnumbered by the once-familiar line up of Class 76 Bo-Bo mixed traffic electrics on 27th June 1981. Since the closure of the 'Woodhead Route' the yard and depot at Wath has fallen into a state of degradation.

## Sheffield Area

In 1870, the Midland Railway opened a direct route via Bradfield Tunnel into Sheffield which was to form the principal MR through route from London to the North. Dore station is situated south of Sheffield where the lines from Derby join the Hope Valley lines from Manchester. Here, a St Pancras-Sheffield IC125 accelerates round the curve from the 2,027 yard long Bradfield Tunnel in August 1983. The Hope Valley lines can be seen in the foreground.

The appearance of Class 50s at Sheffield on a regular basis is unusual, but a relief to the IC125 Penzance-Edinburgh provided occasional haulage from Plymouth to York. Looking more like an enthusiasts' rail tour, the returning Class 50 No.50047 *Swiftsure* heads through Dore station in August 1983. In the background, the line runs downhill to Sheffield, at one time taking in three suburban stations, all served by four tracks, but closed by 1968 as casualties of the Beeching era. Further rationalisation in Feburary 1985 saw the removal of the main line platforms at Dore.

During their final years the Class 40s were widely travelled on freight traffic in the north of England. A regular duty much sought after by photographers was the unusual combination of Class 40 and 25 on the 6441 Bitton-Broughton Lane and return BOC tanks. In this view, Class 40 No.40195 is paired with Class 25 No.25132 on the 15.07 Broughton Lane to Widnes empties near Dore on 23rd June 1984.                    *H. Malham*

Sheffield, world famous for its quality steel products, is the largest city in the Yorkshire region. The opening of Bradfield Tunnel gave Sheffield a direct route from the South to Pond Street station, later to become Sheffield Midland. Over the years, the station has been considerably rebuilt and the contrasting architecture can be seen in this view looking towards the city centre as a pair of IC125s, one in each direction, prepare to depart on the North East-South West service. The IC125s were introduced on the Midland main line in October 1982.

On 26th August 1983, dual-brake Class 37 No.37024 of Tinsley depot made a surprise appearance at Sheffield Midland on the 09.40 Poole-Newcastle having substituted for failed 'Peak' No.45139 at Derby.

Following the elimination of the electric service out of Sheffield Victoria, a curve was opened from the MR line at Nunnery Junction enabling trains from Lincoln and Doncaster to run into Sheffield Midland station. Here, Class 45 No.45183 heads the 10.16 Barrow-Nottingham on the climb from Nunnery Main Line Junction on 29th October 1983. The lines on the right form the Midland route to Leeds and York via Rotherham.

Introduced in 1960, the Swindon-built Class 124 dmus were a stylish addition to the BR fleet for the Trans-Pennine route via Stanhedge. In 1979, the service was restructured with hourly trains composed of air braked-electrically heated Mk 2 coaching stock, and the aged Class 124s were relegated to the south Trans-Pennine route from Hull to Manchester via Doncaster and Sheffield. A distinctive feature of the Trans-Pennine sets was their wrap round windows, seen here as a Class 124 awaits departure on the semi-fast service to Manchester via the Hope Valley line in January 1981.                                        *P. Harris*

In the cavernous gloom of the cutting, headlight blazing, a Romanian-built Class 56 heads towards Tinsley in October 1983. The Class 56s first arrived at Tinsley in 1977.

This formation of departmental stock was observed passing through Sheffield Midland station en route from Wakefield to the Research and Development Division at Derby Technical Centre. Class 31 No.31167 propels Lab 18 RDB 975280 *Mercury* and Lab 17 RDB 975081 *Hermes* with the unusual RDC 460000 structure gauging car in the middle of the set. These vehicles have subsequently been transferred from the Research Department to the Civil Engineers and as a consequence their prefixes amended to DB or DC. On this occasion, the ensemble had probably been assigned to duties on the ECML Selby Coalfield diversion which was nearing completion at the time. *P. Harris*

*Opposite page top:*
One of the legacies left by the early railway builders was their failure to bring all lines to a common terminus in major cities. Leeds, Bradford and Sheffield have undergone radical changes in recent years with hundreds of acres of abandoned railway lines, reduction of used platforms and complete closures of main line passenger stations – the most controversial of which was the decision to withdraw passenger services from the electrified Woodhead route. Here, 'Peak' class No.D62 (later 45143) *5th Royal Inniskilling Dragoon Guards* waits at Sheffield Victoria to take over a Manchester-St Pancras train diverted via Woodhead due to engineering work on 25th August 1969. *Ian S. Carr*

## Sheffield Victoria

*Opposite page bottom:*
The Woodhead Route was electrified by the LNER in 1939 using the Government recommended standard 1,500 volt dc overhead system. The electrification was completed between Manchester and Sheffield in 1955, and extended to the new Tinsley Marshalling Yard ten years later. By then, the equipment was becoming life expired and although several schemes were considered for saving the line, BR opted for re-routing all East-West passenger services across the Pennines via the Hope Valley line, involving closure of Sheffield Victoria station in 1970. Two days before closure, EE Co. Type 3 Co-Co No.D6968 (later 37268) heads the 14.37 Manchester (Piccadilly) to Harwich Parkeston Quay on Saturday 3rd January 1970. This was the last regular trip of the train via Woodhead. *Ian S. Carr*

## Tinsley

Tinsley Marshalling Yard and diesel locomotive depot was part of a multi-million pound freight modernisation scheme announced in 1961 for the Sheffield area. The yard was opened in 1965, covering an area of 145 acres with the capability of handling over 4,000 wagons per day. With the reduction of wagon load traffic and the coincident increase of company trains, history has revealed that Tinsley Yard was outdated almost before it was completed. Today, much of the yard's 60 miles of track has been rendered obsolete, and in 1984 hump marshalling was abandoned and trackwork rationalised to meet new traffic needs. In the twilight of its career, 'Deltic' class No.55013 *The Black Watch* was star attraction at Tinsley's open day. In this view, an invasion of haulage fans say their last adieus, whilst Classes 25, 31, 45 and 47 are paid only scant attention. *P. Harris*

A view of the interior of Tinsley Maintenance Depot; comprised of six bays at each end, with full length raised platforms for ease of access to the traction motors, whilst the lower aisles give side access to bogies and locomotive undergear. During Tinsley's open day, a small boy is dwarfed by the Class 03 shunter and one of the three Class 13 master and slave units, converted from two Class 08s for hump marshalling in the yard and unique to Tinsley. Class 47/0 No.47214 was named *Tinsley Traction Depot* in September 1987 incorporating a new 'White Rose' depot identification plaque beneath the nameplate. *P. Harris*

The initial batch of Romanian and Doncaster-built Class 56s were allocated to Tinsley from 1977. Very much on home territory, Doncaster-built No.56096 stands in the maintenance depot on 27th June 1981. The British-designed Class 56s are easily identified by their modified cab side windows, revised horn grilles, headlight and marker/tail lights. The new livery was applied from No.56084 onwards, including black window surrounds, large BR logo, oversize locomotive number and wrap-round yellow ends.

## Rotherham Area

The major steel producing area of Sheffield and Rotherham is also the centre of the scrap industry. The signalman at Meadow Hall passes over the key to the driver of pilot-scheme veteran Class 20 No.20004, enabling single line occupation and ground frame entrance to Smith's scrap yard at Ecclesfield with T34 from Tinsley Yard. The signal box closed on 4th April 1983.      *J. Wright*

Plate 193
On 25th August 1969, MR passenger traffic was re-routed directly from Rotherham to Chesterfield via Staveley due to engineering work at Broomhouse Tunnel. Passengers for Sheffield had to alight at Rotherham to catch the dmu shuttle to Midland station. With its 55A (Holbeck) shed allocation plate on the nose end, 'Peak' class No.D189 (later 46052) pauses at the now closed Rotherham, Masborough Road station with the 08.20 Newcastle-Bristol.      *Ian S. Carr*

George Cohen's scrap yard lies beside the GC route at Tinsley. In sole charge of shunting is a green liveried 88hp chain driven diesel mechanical shunter, built in 1967 by Ruston & Hornsby (No.513142) at their Lincoln works. In this view, the 7ft 3in low-headroom bridge greatly exaggerates the size of the diminutive 4-wheeled shunter as it drags a load of aged wagons from the yard.

In their final years the Trans-Pennine units were made up of original vehicles, later designated Class 124, together with Class 123s drafted from the WR. Mixed formations were regularly used, however the provision of gangway connections on Swindon's Class 123 gave them an altogether untidy appearance. Here, a 4-car set enters Masborough Road station on the Manchester-Hull service. All train services were diverted from Masborough Road in May 1987 when a new Central station was opened on the GE route. The new service is connected to the Midland route by a newly-constructed curve from Holmes Junction, just south of Rotherham.

*P.Harris*

South Yorkshire is by no means all industry! Passing through some splendid countryside on the GC line near Swinton, Class 45 No.45068 heads a rake of empty bolsters in June 1982. On the right is the Sheffield & South Yorkshire Navigation Canal which had recently undergone a multi-million pound improvement scheme, enabling 700 tonne payload barges as far as Mexborough and 400 tonne barges to Rotherham providing a direct link with the ports of Humberside.

Northwards from Rotherham the MR lines run parallel with the GC lines until both routes meet at the scissors junction at Aldwarke. The NE-SW IC125 s use the junction to cross from the MR lines to the much slower GC Mexborough line on the revised service via Doncaster. Plans to restore a curve north of Swinton will enable faster timings to be obtained from the additional mileage out of Rotherham. With the BSC's plant in the background, including 0-6-0 diesel electric shunter No.95 (Yorkshire 2891 of 1963), Class 47 No.47360 heads northbound at Aldwarke Junction in June 1982.

Equally at home on freight and express trains, the Class 37 is one of the most successful Type 3 locomotives seen on BR lines. With 12-cylinders of EE Co. diesel engines bellowing out, a Class 37 heads through Kilnhurst with empty 77.5 tonne BAA steel-carrying wagons forming the 10.10 SX 6E40 Corby-Lackenby. In the background is the site of Kilnhurst West station which closed in January 1968 when the Leeds-Sheffield local passenger service was withdrawn. *P.Harris*

Framed by the typical GC footbridge, Class 37 No.37048 heads an Orgreave-Scunthorpe mgr on the climb through Conisborough station on 30th August 1983. The station once had three platforms, made up by an island platform on the right for eastbound traffic.

## Doncaster Area

With the Paxman Valenta engines of the IC125's power cars at full cry, a northbound HST accelerates through Doncaster in June 1982. In 1976 revised ECML trackwork was completed, raising the speed limit to 110 mph in the vicinity of Doncaster. Scenes such as this are commonplace, and the adult enthusiast, accused of being trapped in adolescence should be forgiven his benign interest in railways. For me, it evokes memories of the A4 Pacifics during the 1950s when Doncaster became a popular venue for week-end train spotting trips. *P.Harris*

The unmistakable EE Co. lineage can be seen here with two Class 37 variants side by side at Doncaster depot on 14th June 1981. The first 119 locomotives were built with gangway doors and split route indicators each side of the nose, whereas the remainder of the class were built with a centrally positioned headcode panel and roof mounted warning horns.

A green oasis within the BREL campus with a Class 08 shunter and the then newly-built Class 58 No.58002 on 13th May 1983. Completion of this, the second Class 58 to be built at Doncaster enabled multiple-control and slow speed testing to be carried out with No.58001. The striking 'Railfreight' livery applied to the Class 58 was a welcome change from the drab overall blue of the Corporate Identity scheme. Variations in new colour schemes are now commonplace and clearly shows BRB's intention to improve its hitherto unglamorous image for main line train liveries.

Since the arrival of the GNR in 1849, Doncaster has had a long history as a railway town. The famous 'Plant' locomotive works was established in 1853, working under the direction of many well-known Chief Mechanical Engineers whose reputations are synonymous with the locomotive types that came off the assembly line. The post of CME was abolished following Nationalisation, and in 1968 British Rail Engineering Limited was formed. With the BREL offices visible in the background, Class 40 No.40069 heads a train of tank wagons on the Sheffield line in August 1983.

*Opposite page, top:* The Class 56s were the first main line diesel locomotives to be ordered since the 1960s. Built specifically for heavy freight duties throughout the BR network, the first 30 locomotives were subcontracted by Brush to the Electroputere Works in Romania and were delivered to BR in August 1976. Unfortunately, their introduction was unsatisfactory in many respects when they failed to meet BR's exacting specifications. From such an unauspicious start however, the Class 56s have become the regular workhorses of the BR fleet. The exposed girders at Doncaster depot cast light and shade on Romanian built Nos 56005 and 56028 on 5th June 1983.

*Opposite page, bottom:* Letting off steam in the repair shop at Doncaster, Class 40 No.40013 *Andania* gives a good impression of the atmosphere to be found at Doncaster's former steam shed on 4th June 1981. Although officially withdrawn in January 1985, this locomotive, alias No.D213 was taken into custody at Tyseley depot and re-painted in various guises of green livery, including at one time white cab surrounds ('Deltic' style) for its use as a non-working exhibition locomotive and static display at LMR open days. It has now been acquired for preservation and restoration to working order.

The Sheffield-based company of Cravens Ltd built a total of 405 railcars, including 278 powered vehicles. They were delivered from 1956 and allocated initially to Springhead depot, and then Botanic Gardens on North Humberside. A distinctive feature of the Class 105 is the two large windows, seen clearly in this fine study of a 2-car set awaiting departure from Doncaster on the night of 30th November 1979. Note the blanked-off top marker light and stencilled 'LW' for 'lightweight' over the buffer beam.

*P.Harris*

# The 'Plant'

*Opposite page, top:* Steam enthusiasts will derive some melancholy satisfaction from the sight of a diesel in such a lamentable state of disrepair! At the end of its days, 'Toffee Apple' Class 31/0 cabs have been dumped unceremoniously at the back of the 'abattoir' on 14th June 1981. The nickname of the Class 31/0s was derived from the unusual shape of their control desk power handles, now no longer required as the cab shells await another Class 31 to sustain damage and requiring a transplant. The Class 31, alias No.D5505, was one of the original batch of 20 pilot scheme locomotives ordered as part of the Modernisation Plan. All have been scrapped, except for No.D5500 now preserved at the National Railway Museum.

*Opposite page, bottom:* A decade of main line running had taken its toll on the Class 50s, and by the late 1970s locomotive failures were commonplace. The multi-million pound refurbishing programme which was started in 1979 was essentially a complete rebuild of the fleet. The work included removal of the rheostatic brakes and slow speed control, modification of brake cylinders, re-equipping the main electrical equipment and overhaul of the EE 16-cylinder CVST turbo-charged power units. The appearance of the outshopped 50s showed little sign of the massive undertaking, except for a circular hole cut into the cab fronts for a high density headlight, and the redundant headcode panels which were replaced by translucent marker discs. In addition, the recessed roof line was repanelled to accommodate a new roof fan, whilst to a lesser extent a small bodyside window was replaced by a grille to improve air intake. Up to three Class 50s stood on the erecting shop floor at one time, and in this 14th June 1981 view, all work can be seen in progress as No.50045 *Achilles* shares company with No.50033 *Glorious* and No.50039 *Implacable*.

*Below:* December 1982 heralded the unveiling of BREL Doncaster's latest product in the shape of the Class 58 locomotive. The building of the class was different from traditional designs in having a simple underframe with a non-load bearing superstructure. It led to a big saving in construction costs compared with the normal monocoque type of earlier designs. Here, No.58019 is at an advanced stage of construction in the main erecting shops and shows the 12-cylinder development of the Ruston-Paxman engine. Completion of the Class 58s has seen the end of more than a century of locomotive building in the town. To reduce its maintenance bill, BREL was split into two parts, and Doncaster Works has now become part of a new subsidiary – BR Maintenance Ltd, which is dedicated to routine maintenance and light overhauls.

*P.Harris*

Following a collision with coaching stock at Bristol, Class 50 No.50044 *Exeter* was despatched to Doncaster BREL for repairs. The outshopped Class 50 was returned to the WR most unusually on the 09.10 Scunthorpe CHP – Severn Tunnel Junction mgr empties on 31st August 1983. With the towering chimneys of Doncaster Power Station dominating the background, *Exeter* heads onto the main line during a test run on 29th August.

It is amazing the lengths to which some graffiti artists will go to find an outlet for their work! A candidate for treatment is the rail bridge at Conisbrough which carries the Doncaster-Mexborough line over the River Don, seen here suitably daubed by local youths as Class 40 No.40044 heads the Cleethorpes-Red Bank parcels in May 1982. On the left are empty mgr hoppers in the now closed NCB Cadeby Colliery sidings.                               *P.Harris*

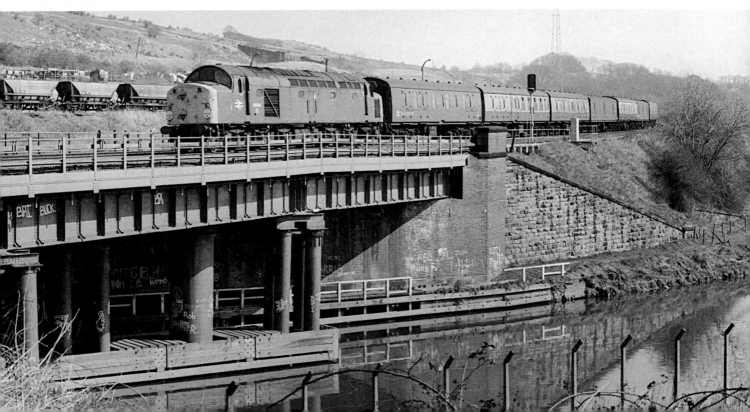

The warbling whistle of 16 English Electric cylinders rises to a crescendo of sound as veteran Class 40 No.40024 *Lucania* restarts the Cleethorpes-Red Bank parcel train at Doncaster. The Class 40, originally No.D224, was one of 25 EE Co. Type 4s allocated to the LM Region which received names of great Trans-Atlantic liners associated with the port of Liverpool. From 1970, the attractive cast metal plates were removed, leaving only a group of bolts to mark their bodyside position. Certain examples had their names revived in white stencilled letters, as did this one. The name *Lucania* was derived from a region of southern Italy and was bestowed on a 12,900 ton ocean liner belonging to the Cunard Steamship Company.

*P.Harris*

This view of Doncaster is already consigned to history with the appearance of 25kV overhead line equipment and Class 91 'Electras'. Although BR's flagship IC125s are gradually being phased out from the ECML, the impact of the fleet over the past ten years has provided a sound business base to justify expenditure on electrification. With the BREL (now BR Maintenance Ltd) works in the background, a northbound IC125 heads non-stop through Doncaster in August 1983. Standing in West Yard are condemned Class 306 emus awaiting scrapping. Several of the derelict units languished at Doncaster for some time before removal to Horwich for breaking up.

On 22nd October 1983, the early morning sun penetrates the mist rising from hoarfrost across Doncaster Carr Sidings. In the left background, Landore based Class 37 No.37180 *Sir Dyfed/County of Dyfed* heads south on the main line with the 08.37 Leeds-King's Cross relief. The Class 37 failed at Peterborough on a return working later that day.

The introduction of block trainloads has seen the demise of loose-coupled rail wagon loads, particularly in the movement of coal. The empty sidings at Stainforth reveal the extent of Hatfield's coal wagon traffic, now displaced by the merry-go-round concept with its continuous circuit operation from pit to power station and automatic loading/unloading at terminals. Class 47 No.47371 heads through Stainforth with mgr empties for Dearne Valley Colliery. The NCB's Hatfield Colliery can be seen in the background.

With early morning frost still clinging to the permanent way, a Goole-Doncaster 2-car Metro-Cammell unit accelerates away from Stainforth & Hatfield station on 22nd October 1983. A medium telephoto lens accentuates the ladder junction and freight-only lines to Knottingley and Wakefield on the right.

# Deltics – The End of an Era

In its smart, but unorthodox blue livery, the prototype 'Deltic' heads the 13.35 to King's Cross out of Doncaster on 26th February 1959. Built in 1955 by English Electric, *Deltic* was powered by two Napier 18-cylinder 1,650bhp engines giving a total of 3,300bhp. It weighed 106 tons and had a maximum tractive effort of 60,000lb – at the time, the most powerful single-unit diesel electric locomotive in the world. The American-style nose with its large headlight can be seen clearly. The headlight was never used, and the locomotive usually carried two oil lamps above the buffer beam which was adopted from the traditional headlamp code of the steam era.  *BR*

During the 1960s, nobody would have believed that a diesel locomotive would be worshipped with all the fanaticism of its steam predecessor, yet by the 1980s the 'Deltics' were treated with all the reverence we thought was only reserved for the Gresley Pacifics they had displaced. *(Above)* Working flat out on the GN line between Carcroft and Hampole, No.D9017 *The Durham Light Infantry* heads a Leeds-King's Cross express towards Doncaster on 4th April 1964. In the opposite direction, *(Opposite page, top)* No.D9011 *The Royal Northumberland Fusiliers* heads the 'down' "Queen of Scots" Pullman in typical flamboyant style.

*Both: M. Mitchell*

On 27th February 1982, some employees at BREL Doncaster arranged a restricted 'Farewell to the Deltic' open day with proceeds going to charity. It compelled several thousand enthusiasts to pay their last respects to these fine machines. Of the 19 locomotives on display, three 'Deltics' had their engines operational, including No.55002 on loan from the NRM, and the Deltic Preservation Society's future purchases Nos 55009 and 55019. Despite the graffiti artist's plea of "Save me", no such luck awaited No.55010. Distinguished as the first 'Deltic' to achieve 2 million miles, but now looking a little worse for wear, and shorn of its *The King's Own Scottish Borderer* nameplates which were presented to the regiment by BR.

## The Second Generation dmus

When BR realised that their present stock of dmus, built to designs conceived during the 1950s, were rapidly wearing out en masse, it was decided to embark on a programme of almost total replacement of its existing fleet. The BR/Leyland narrow bodied Class 141 was the first of the second generation diesel units introduced to traffic in West Yorkshire on 18th April 1984. The design is made up of a pair of 4-wheeled vehicles with a body built at British Leyland's bus works at Workington. Before the service commenced drivers familiarised themselves with the new vehicles on a training run between York and Leeds, and set No.141003 is seen at Church Fenton in January 1984. The introduction of the Class 141 was dogged by troublesome transmission and in particular poor brakes which caused the vehicles to slide when braking. Within a few weeks of service Neville Hill's drivers had christened them "Torville & Dean's"!

Similar to the Class 141 is the Class 142 2-car, wider-bodied 'Pacer' variant, for local and secondary services. The sets consist of a bus body built at British Leyland Workington mounted on a 4-wheeled underframe built at Derby. Here, front end comparisons can be made between the two designs outside the dmu repair shop at Neville Hill depot, Leeds. The variation in coupling height between the two classes is clearly seen; the Class 141's non-compatible tightlock type and the now-standard BSI automatic coupler of the 142, which enables multiple unit operation with other second generation vehicles.

Today there has emerged two different types of second generation dmus. First, the railbus – essentially a bus body on a rail chassis and designated the Class 14X 'Pacer' series, whilst the Class 15X 'Sprinters' are a high technology Mk 3 coach body shell with diesel engines slung beneath. *Above:* BR's coat of many colours at Leeds with a Class 141 on the left in the much-maligned light green and cream livery of the new WYPTE and the Class 144 in the new Metrotrain livery of crimson and cream. In the background are Class 142 units and recently erected catenary support masts for the ECML electrification scheme. *Below:* A product of York BREL and successor to their Class 150/1 'Sprinter' is the 2-car Class 150/2s. Compared with the front-end styling of the Class 150/1, (see inset back cover) the revised cab design with corridor connections enables access between sets when two or more sets are coupled together for the Provincial Sector's longer distance services.

Since the beginning of the 1987 summer timetable, the second generation dmus have taken over almost all rural services in the Yorkshire region. The twin railbuses built by W.Alexander/A.Barclay were designated Class 143 and made their debut in 1985 for use in the Tyneside area. Here, Nos 143019 and 143024 making up the 07.23 Middlesbrough-Whitby are seen running alongside the River Esk at Whitby in June 1987. The leading set is one of the six Class 143s painted in the Tyne & Wear PTE's livery of yellow and white, whereas the trailing unit is finished in the new Provincial Sector two-tone blue livery. The good looks of the new vehicles are let down by the design of their interiors, particularly the solid bulkheads behind the driver's cab which denies passengers both front and rear views over some of the most picturesque lines which BR are seeking to promote.

Emerging from the post-beeching doldrums of the 1960s, BR's Passenger and Railfreight Sectors have entered a new era. Unfortunately, BR were unable to avoid some similar mistakes to those that occurred during the 1955 Modernisation Plan when large numbers of unsuitable designs were introduced. The Advanced Passenger Train, "APT" smacked once again of the well documented list of failures and costly writing off although many useful lessons were learnt. The APT-E (two gas turbine power cars and two trailers forming the pre-production prototype) arrived at York on 11th June 1976 and put on temporary display out of doors. Here, the sleek nose is shown to good effect inside the roundhouse of the National Railway Museum.

*P.Harris*